Fire Up Your Photo & Bio

Grab Fans *BEFORE* They See Your Work

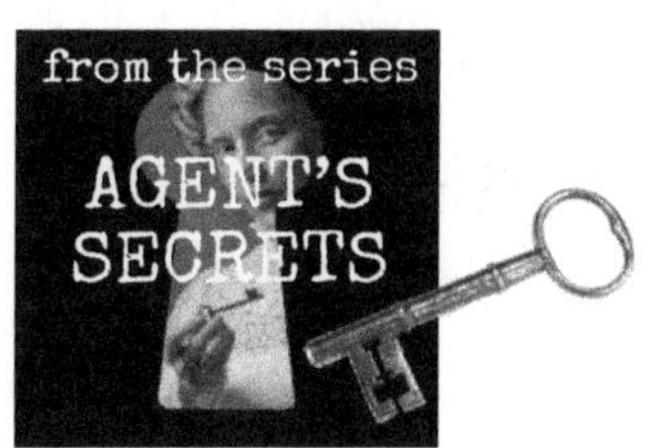

CRICKET FREEMAN

AUGUST WORDS PUBLISHING!
unique books by exceptional authors for select readers

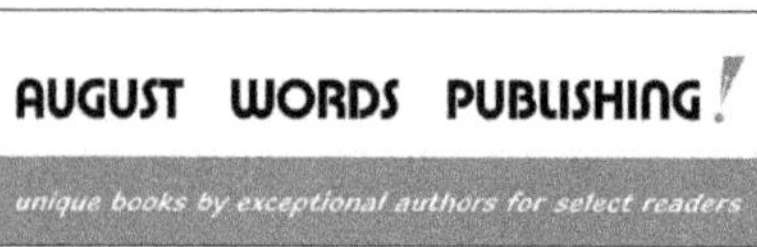

Published by
August Words Publishing
www.AugustWordsPublishing.com

Cover design	The August Agency LLC
Book design	The August Agency LLC
Cover photos	Historic images
Interior photos	Library of Congress, WikiCommons
Author photo	Bill Freeman

ISBN: 978-1-942018-21-6

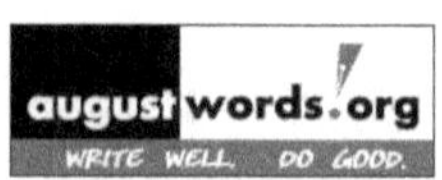

Dedication

To my dear B Free,
who taught me to fully
embrace the philosophy.

"Twenty years from now you will be more disappointed by the things you didn't do than by the ones you did do. So, throw off the bowlines. Sail away from the safe harbor. Catch the trade winds in your sails. Explore. Dream. Discover."

~ Mark Twain

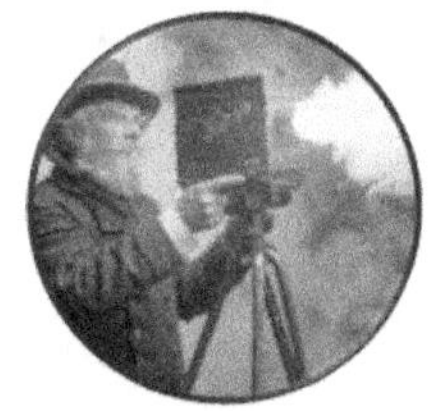

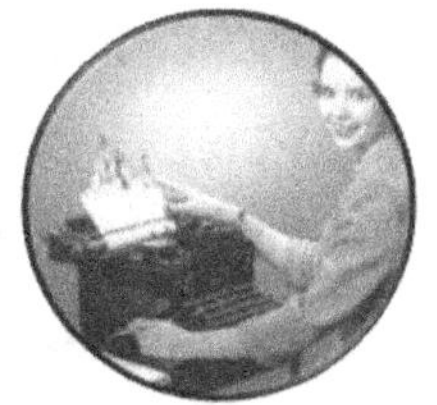

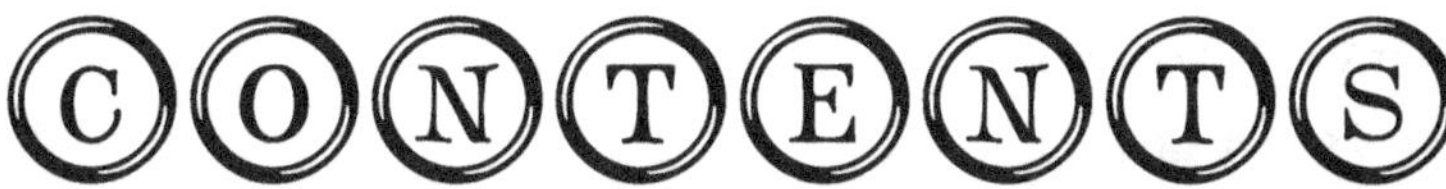

CONTENTS

"As you search for a place to enter the untamed forest, don't settle for a well-trodden path. Don't settle down, don't settle in, don't settle."

~ Richard Krevolin

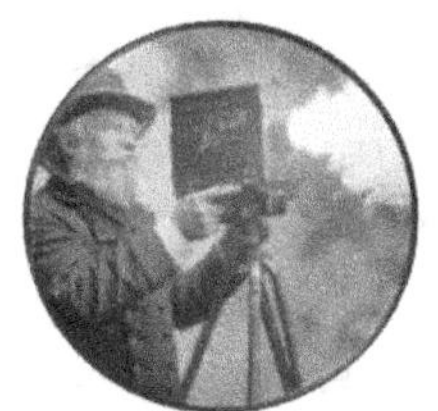

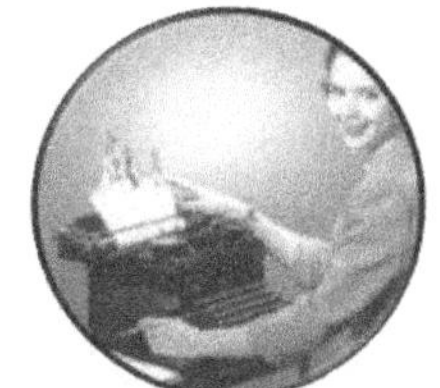

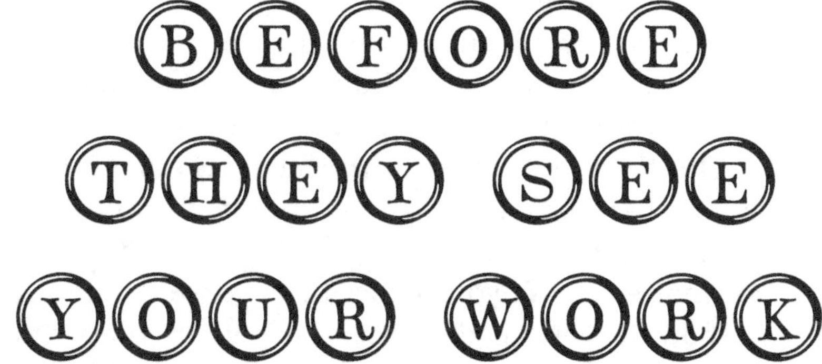

BEFORE THEY SEE YOUR WORK

Whether you are an Author, Content Creator, Host, Influencer, Blogger, Artist, Commentator, Video Creator, Podcaster, Writer, Musician, Reporter, Reviewer, or today's Social Media Maven – any of our self-applied designations we employ to describe what it is we do – we are social communicators. We have opinions, ideas, beliefs, philosophies, and theories of the world, and we communicate our viewpoint through our work. (Personally, as a Writer I prefer the stamp of Word Warrior; it seems to sum up the attitude I need on those tough days when I must channel my inner Wonder Woman to deal with a fickle, mutinous Muse.)

As contributors to how society regards itself, we are blessed with an incredible gift. The gift of glorious gab. We speak through our work. This is no small thing, my friends.

Think about what it is you do when you express yourself through your work: You take the feelings in your heart, convey them to your brain, then to your mouth or fingertips to be articulated in your work – where your Readers, Listeners, or Viewers pick them up through their ears and eyes, and convey them to their brains and, if you're as good as you should be, then those feelings touch their hearts, carrying the same feelings as in yours.

Yes, indeed, your gift of gab is rare. Not every Tom, Dick, and Hermoine has the ability to express themselves through their work. Respect your gift. Learn to use it wisely. Truth be told, there are others with this glorious gift of gab – some better than others – so be mindful, you do have competition out there, Kiddo.

No matter how you describe yourself, there's no question about it, you need to rise above your competition if you wish to connect with your Readers, Viewers, Listeners – and convert them to your Tried-and-True Fans.

You need to grab their attention from the get-go and never let go. You need to tantalize them. Draw them in. Captivate them. Have them feel a connection.

And in this world, let's be honest here, you have, *MAYBE*, three seconds to do that as they scroll through masses of content online. And, *WOW*, you have only one shot before they're on to the next thing vying for their attention, probably never to return again.

Any one of them could become a Fan. Think about that for a moment. Anyone who sees only Your Photo or Your Bio will, in a nanosecond, decide if they will connect or not. With just Your Photo and Bio, you could grab them – *BEFORE* they've read the first word from your beautiful, blistering pen; seen any of your amazing, groundbreaking work; or heard the first word from your awesome, *au courant* lips.

It is a tall order – but it is exactly what your Photo and Bio are designed to do. To connect.

Look at it this way: Your Photo is your handiest, legit, major mondo, A-number-1, indispensable, hardest-working secret weapon, promoting piece-of-wizardry Monetizer. And your Bio is close behind.

Yeah, that's putting a lot into two small packages, but I can help: I'll dish up the straight skinny, and show you how to pull it all out, morsel-by-crumb.

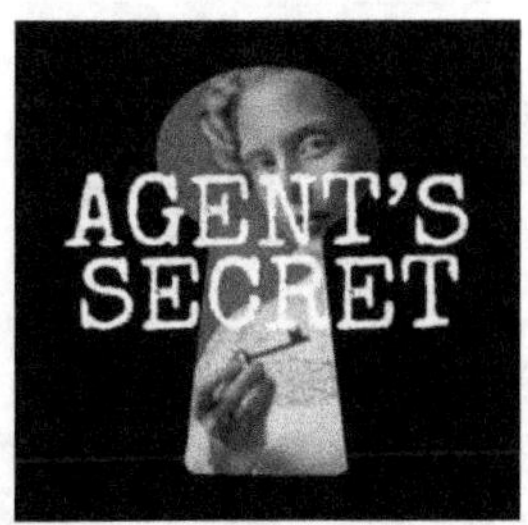

Your Photo is NOT a stock headshot.

Your Bio is NOT a biography.
Nor a lifeless resumé.

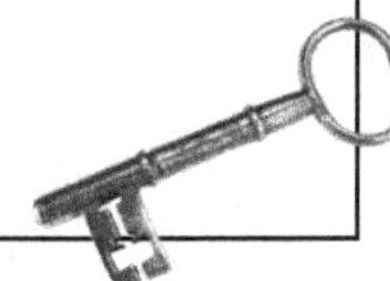

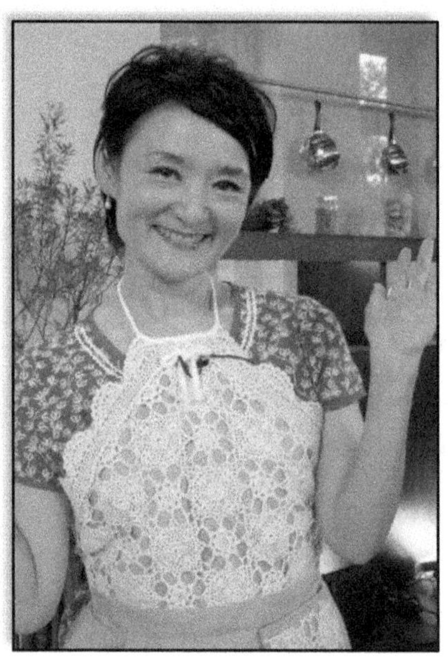

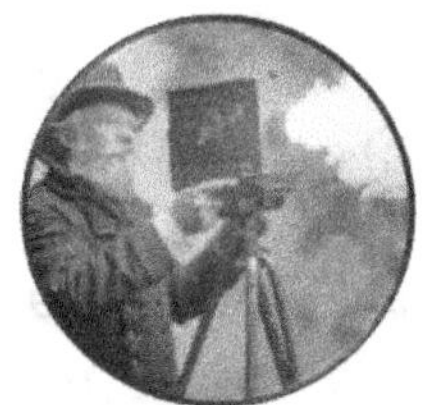

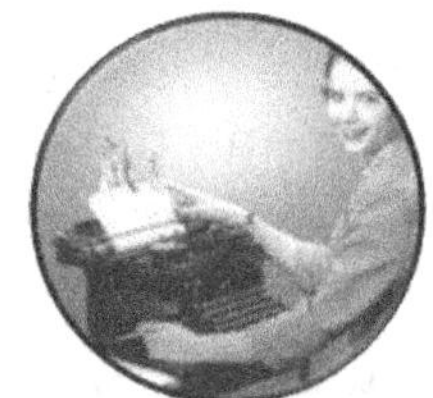

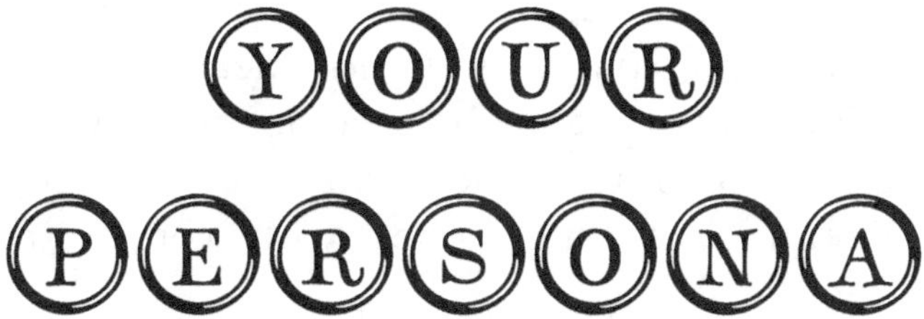

Your Persona

To connect with Readers, Viewers, Listeners, you will need to develop and fine tune a separate, well-thought-out, defined, detailed Persona. This is you: Your Persona, The Author, The Host, The Influencer, The Reviewer, The Artist. You, The Authority. You'll roll out Your Persona whenever you need to present a public face for your audience.

You're already familiar with the concept. You're a different Persona at work than you are with your friends, your lover, your parents, aren't you? OK. The Persona you wish to present to your Fans is just one more version of yourself.

Remember, Your Persona is you, but not you. Your Photo is where Fans first see Your Persona and size you up and Your Bio is where they get to know you through a description of Your Persona.

You're striving for love at first sight.

To start with, think deeply about who you want Your Persona to be. Who that is – and isn't. This is not something you can leave to happenstance. It must be carefully considered and curated for optimum results. Your Persona must be someone your target audience will respond to, someone who is totally authentic. No liars, charlatans, frauds, fakers, or phonies here.

Because, most significantly, Your Persona must be someone your Fans trust, trust to not cheat them somewhere down the line. Your Persona is someone your Fans have confidence in, enough to connect with. So much so, they will want to spend time and money with you. Repeatedly. Consistently.

It is simpler – and yet, somehow, harder – than you may think.

You are an enthusiast, engaged in what you're passionate about, doing what you love. Take that and express yourself. Use your own distinctive voice. Don't hold back. Bring out your own special style. Be open. Be expansive. Roll out the old razzle-dazzle. Be your own original, clever, nerdy self. Let your freak flag fly.

Just be yourself, Honey – totally. Be your True You.

I do realize some of you learned as a kid to restrain your True You because revealing it drew school bullies like heat-seeking missiles. But it's time to put on your big boy or big girl pants and power through it. It is time to embrace your True You.

Wrap your creativity into defining Your Persona. Fold all of that True You – beautifully, elegantly, authentically – into Your Persona.

Fans want to connect with you, and you can use Your Persona to connect with them. Through story. Through emotion.

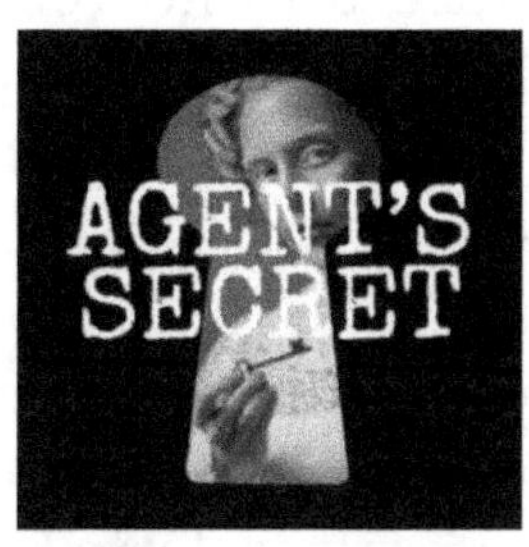

Emotion is craved.
It is Mother's Milk.
It is Heart Support.
It is Muscle Drive.
It is Electric Power.
It is Atomic Fuel.

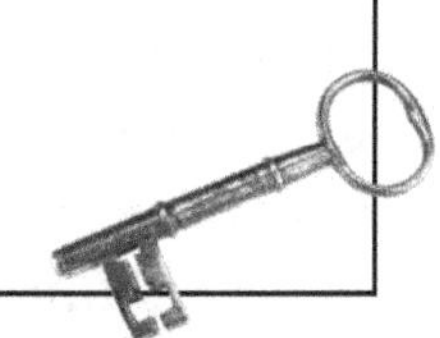

Mull over and plan what story you wish to convey, what emotion you want to express through Your Persona, what would resonate with Fans. Hard, soft, knowledgeable, clever, passionate, opinionated, energetic, funny, rugged, dedicated, experienced, romantic, sardonic, sympathetic, snarky. Or maybe a combo platter. You figure out what best defines the Persona you wish to present to the world.

Think of ways to imaginatively illustrate your preferred emotions in Your Photo. Use your outfit, body language, expressions, props, backdrop, location.

If you create quirky works, then, an unconventional, experimental, or wacky Persona and pose in Your Photo could be appropriate, such as an unexpected expression, an off-the-wall outfit, or zany location. But if you need to appear authoritative for your chosen target audience, then Your Persona certainly requires professionalism and sincerity in Your Photo in your choice of expression, outfit, and setting.

Once you've firmed up who Your Persona is, you will need to think about how you want to portray Your Persona consistently in public. Take the time to consider and select a standard outfit that characterizes Your Persona and the story you wish to tell.

When you consistently show up as Your Persona in person, in interviews, or online, your Fans will grow to identify you easily by your selected outfit, Your Persona Uniform. They'll perk up and pay attention, primed for the latest thing you have to say.

Your Persona Uniform could be anything from a Hawaiian shirt and khakis to a suit, or jeans and hoodie to pearls and heels. Just be sure it exemplifies Your Persona and respects your audience. Also, be sure it is versatile, makes you comfortable in all kinds of situations and conditions, and you consistently wear it when assuming your role in public.

Simple clothes and solid-colored fabrics contrast with nearly any backdrop and photograph well. Classic styles are always tasteful and will still look good in a few years, avoiding having to have a new Photo just because your outfit is shockingly out of style. Choose colors that are flattering to your complexion and contrast with any backgrounds in Your Photo.

A crisp, starched, white dress shirt against a dark background always looks good on everyone – man, woman, child, redhead, or Romulan. It works well in color or black and white shots. Variations can include cotton, silk, denim, even leather. Cuffs buttoned down, folded back, or rolled up.

Alternately, a simple, black turtleneck works against a light background – it sure carried the day for Steve Jobs. And it always works well in color and black and white shots, too. Light cotton, heavy cable knit. Sleeves down or pushed up.

And now, I must say a few words about hats.... I know, some of you think it's the best way to distinguish yourself from everyone else. Well, it will, but usually not in a way you'd hope, or expect. Somehow, they just rarely work, especially on women. If you wear one in Your Photo you run the risk of looking like you're trying too hard. Plus, it is always difficult to get a good, flattering shot without shadows trailing across your face. To be on the safe side, to be taken seriously by your Viewers, Listeners, or Readers, only wear a hat if it relates directly to Your Persona. For instance, such as a hard hat if you host construction videos, a cowboy hat if you write westerns, a ball cap if your work involves sports, or, of course, a turban if you are Sikh. All of those represent a distinctive part of Your Persona. Otherwise, play it safe and avoid any form of a hat.

For various occasions, backdrops, or weather conditions, you'll want several versions of your Uniform, in different fabrics, weights, colors. But be sure each of them still conveys Your Persona. For example, a blazer can be in many fabrics and colors, dressed up or down, lighter or heavier, for any occasion, but still be the Persona they expect.

The best part of having a pre-selected Persona Uniform is that anytime you need to go to work, you can easily slip into Your Persona simply by putting it on.

A wonderfully entertaining, almost over-the-top example of a finely-articulated Persona and his Persona Uniform is the late Martin Caidin. Beginning as an on-air network TV Reporter during the U.S. Space Program and the U.S.-Soviet Cold War, once the U.S. reached the moon, he shifted his focus to write dozens of adventure novels, including *Cyborg,* the basis for the successful "Six-Million-Dollar Man" and "Bionic Woman" TV series, plus *Marooned,* the book made into an Academy-Award-winning movie.

Once he became an adventure Author, Martin shifted his Public Persona from coat-and-tie TV Reporter to a quirky, Indiana Jones-type Adventurer. On more than one occasion when I was in his home, lunchtime would roll around and he'd say, "Let's go get some bar-b-que." But before we could venture into public he'd have to change out of our standard South Florida Uniform of Hawaiian shirt, shorts, and sandals and into his Martin Caidin, Author Uniform: jeans, safari shirt, battle-fatigued boots, battered leather vest, crumpled broad-brimmed hat on his totally-shaved head, big fat cigar, huge smile, and, of course, a single gold skull earring with diamond eyes and a ruby mouth.

However, not everyone can pull off that level of role playing, with the outfit to suit, nor has the dedication to maintain it, but it seemed to come easily to Marty. And you certainly had to admire his showmanship; he achieved his goal. Everyone always broke out in a warm smile the moment they saw him, eager to hear about his latest book.

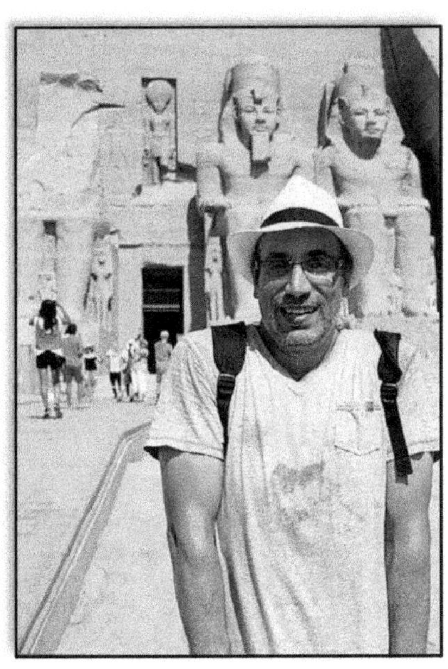

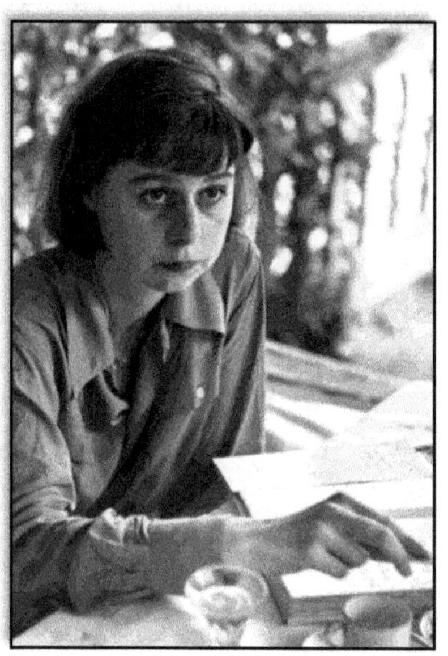

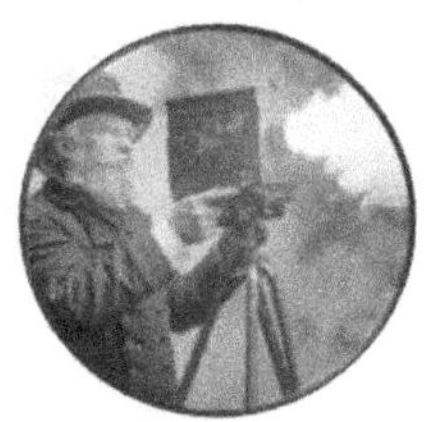

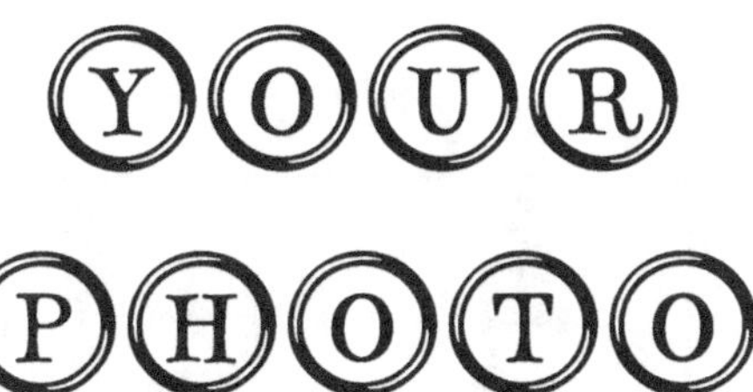
YOUR
PHOTO

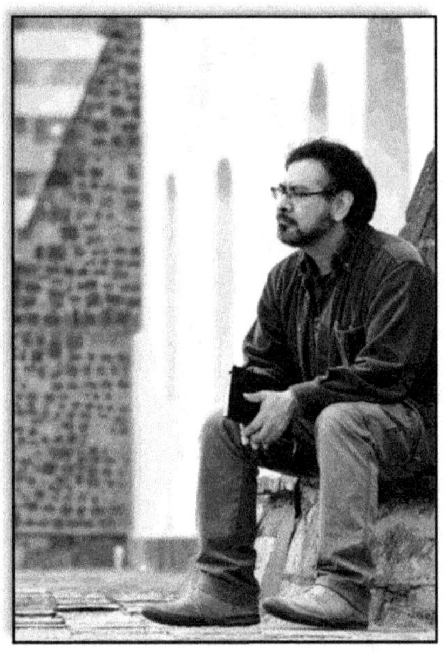

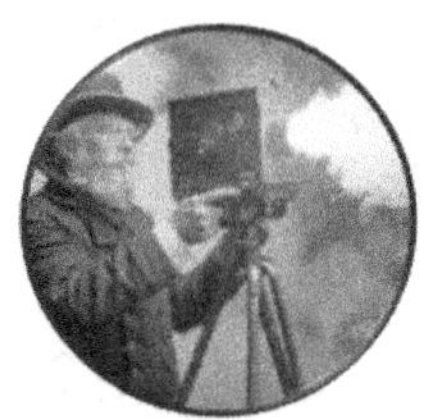

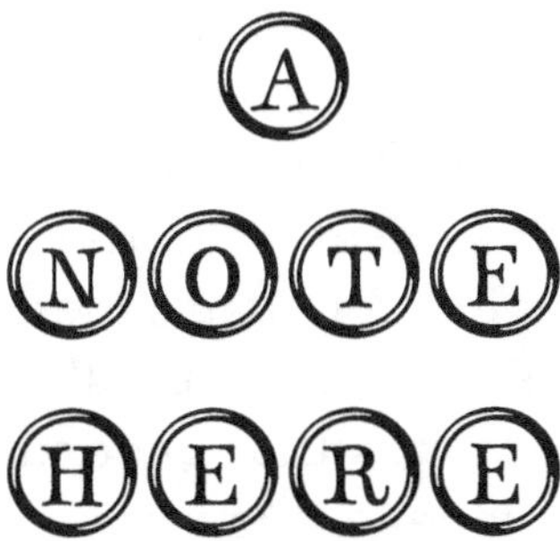

A NOTE HERE

About a zillion years ago, when I was a blazingly-young college student (still a teenager, in fact), I found myself married to what turned out to be my Practice Husband, a photography student at the University. So, I was there, too, following him about like a devoted little puppy.

Between my own undergraduate classes, I would sit in on all his advanced photography classes, just hanging out in a corner, eavesdropping, soaking it all in by sheer osmosis. Some of the time I didn't understand the underlying basics of what they were talking about, but I filled in the missing pieces as I went.

The knowledge I absorbed turned out to be a huge stroke of luck, a blessing I later would come to appreciate. Knowledge is like that. Sneaks up on you. Often gained when you least expect it.

As all of this flowed in and bounced around my hungry brain, I absorbed the ins, outs, compositions, structures, realities, trickeries, twists, and bendings of photography from the best of the best, including surrealist Photographer Jerry Uelsmann (Museum of Modern Art, Metropolitan Museum of Art, Whitney Museum of American Art, Getty Museum, Victoria and Albert Museum, and more).

Just being there, in those muggy classrooms and cool darkrooms, sucking up theory and practice, would set me up for every photo I took for the rest of my life.

For many years I beat back the wolf at my door as a full-time freelance writer for magazines, funding everything from groceries to gas. Serendipitously, it was the photos I took to illustrate my stories that padded my paycheck nicely enough so that occasionally there was cake.

Then, later, as a writer for businesses, my now-pricey photos filled my clients' brochures, manuals, ads, articles, videos, and commercials. And there was more cake, more often.

As an Editor of a national, full-color slick monthly trade magazine, I went from taking photos to editing and curating them.

Later as a small Publisher, the responsibility fell to me to edit and curate the photos that would grace the covers of the books we published, knowing that, yes, indeed, Readers choose a book based mostly on its cover.

However, the time spent in those university classrooms and darkrooms became the most valuable once I became a Literary Agent, representing Writers to Publishers. In the thousands of submissions I've reviewed, every conceivable Author Photo crossed my desk, from boring, forgettable headshots to, OMG, a naked, wrinkly old dude playing basketball (I mean, you just can't unsee that.)

As a Literary Agent I could then take all that initial knowledge I gained from those early days in muggy classrooms and cool darkrooms, and experience over the years, with what worked and what didn't, and adapt it for my clients. I could direct my clients to create dynamic Author Photos to showcase their own unique Author Persona, and capture Fans.

Now, I can direct the same knowledge and experience to direct you to use your creativity to produce Your Photo showcasing Your Persona and capture your Fans.

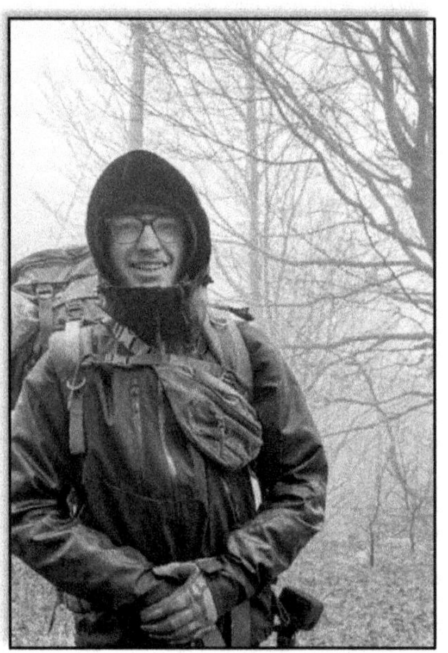

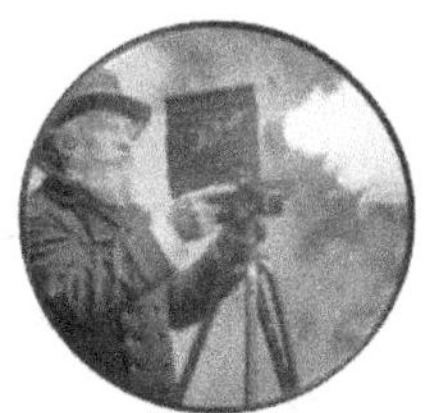

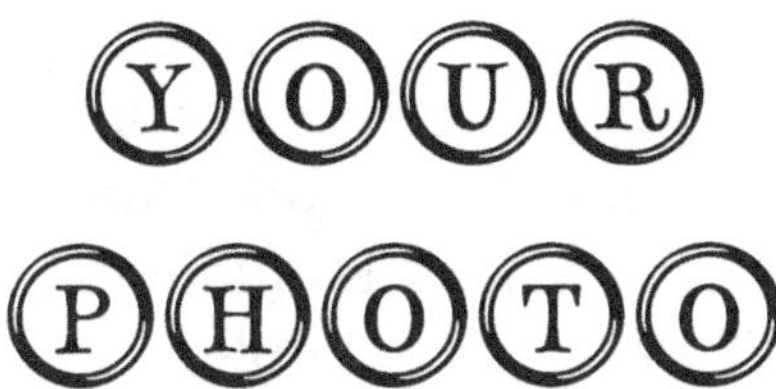

YOUR PHOTO

Your Photo is the best tool in your toolbox for you to attract your audience, whether they are Readers, Viewers, or Listeners. Then to convert them to your biggest Fans.

So, you say, "What's the big deal? You can get a headshot anywhere, anytime. Anything will do."

But a lovely headshot isn't enough, is it?

No.

An emphatic *NO*, Honey.

It is so much more. It *MUST* be – if you want those Fans to experience your work.

If your Viewers, Listeners, Readers, take one look at Your Photo and feel some rapport with Your Persona, you'll make that desired connection in an instant.

A photo is direct. It's fast. It's efficient. It's effective. It's chock full of information. Your Photo needs to be all of that – and more. A picture is worth a thousand words, right? It's a cliché, sure, but clichés become clichés by being starkly, repeatedly, true.

Your Photo is aimed specifically at your intended audience. Think hard and long about who they are, and what you want them to feel, so that with one look they instantly know they want to connect with you, enter your world, take a trip with you, and you are their trusted guide.

Let's talk about the shot itself. Basics first. Don't think Your Photo is anything like a photo for your sweetheart, Granny, or dating app, either. Definitely do not think about using a 20-year-old fuzzy vacation snapshot because you like how sincere/skinny/sexy you look. And AI... Oh, don't get me started... In fact, you'll reek of fakery.

For most Photos, the simpler, the better. Keep in mind, you may wish to have several, depending on where it is being used. For instance, if it's for a book jacket, website, or promo poster, you'll have lots of space to tell your story in Your Photo. If it's a teeny on-line icon, you'll need a very tight crop of your face.

You want to show the world how attractive you are, right? Of course. Trust me, you're not aiming for pretty here. You don't want to *LOOK* attractive; you want to *BE* attractive.

To help you define what type of shot you think might best define Your Persona, and attract Fans, plow through Contributor Photos in your favorite social media, haunt YouTube channel icons, or simply search online for "author photos," clicking through dozens of photos. What catches your eye? Where do your eyes land? Which ones remind you of Your Persona? Which ones convey emotions similar to those you wish to convey? Which can you borrow from? Which ones can you emulate in your own style?

Remember, you and the whole world will be looking at Your Photo for years to come – invest the time and effort to get the best ones you can. It's an investment in yourself. I ask you: Do you know of a better one?

Here are a few descriptions of effective Photos, some from friends and clients:

- A Podcaster on her Harley. Listeners can feel like they'll be going on an exciting journey with her.
- A four-time Author at a booksigning, head down, book open, pen in hand, mid-autograph. It defines success, implying his books are worth the reader's time and money.
- A Poet in a closely-cropped, intimate headshot. This shows Readers they'll get up close and personal, deep into the Author's emotions.
- A Native-American writing team, Activists, under a tree with their pet wolf seated beside them.
- A novelist in front of a famous stadium, as his plots always entangled players in difficult situations.
- A travel Influencer on her sailboat, leaning away from the mast, into the wind.
- A Reporter on the steps of a government building, running up the steps, eager to get that breaking story for his Fans.
- A sports Commentator on a golf course green, grabbing and pulling the flag out of the hole.
- An Author on her back stoop, clutching her coffee cup. It shows she's a regular gal, just like her Readers, someone they can relate to, someone they'd like to join for conversation over coffee.
- A bestselling crime Novelist in front of one of the iconic locations in his successful series.
- A Musician silhouetted against a turbulent sea, looking off into the distance. It's so delightfully metaphoric and sensual, showing lots of textures and soft movement from the ocean and the wind.

- An erotic thriller Writer sitting on a sand dune in his jeans and white dress shirt, the top buttons undone, one knee bent, bare feet in the sand, leaning forward, staring straight into the lens, disarming the viewer.
- A young guy, a Writer of chick lit, worried he'd lose his audience if they knew his books were written by a guy, got creative. His Author Photo was a young woman coming through a screened door, her head turned away from the camera, a curly-headed toddler on her hip staring intently into the camera – he was the toddler. As a special touch he used his mother's Irish name as his pen name, Erin. The young women at his booksignings and on social media adored sharing in the sleight-of-hand.

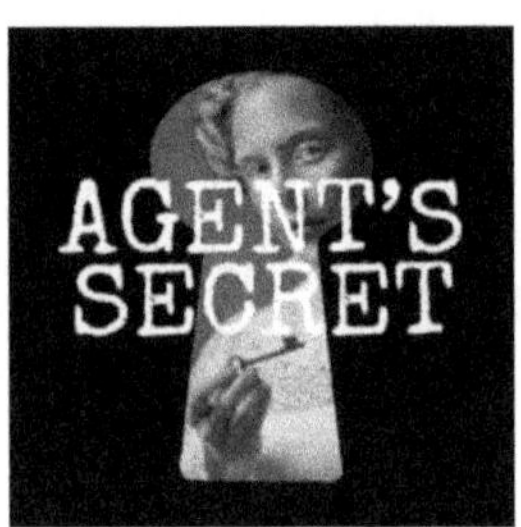

Your Photo is a portrait of Your Persona.

It is not Norma Jean.
It is Marilyn.

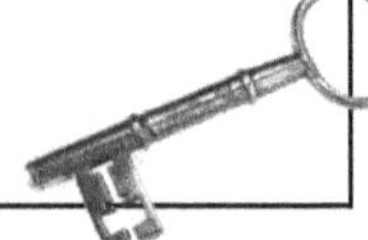

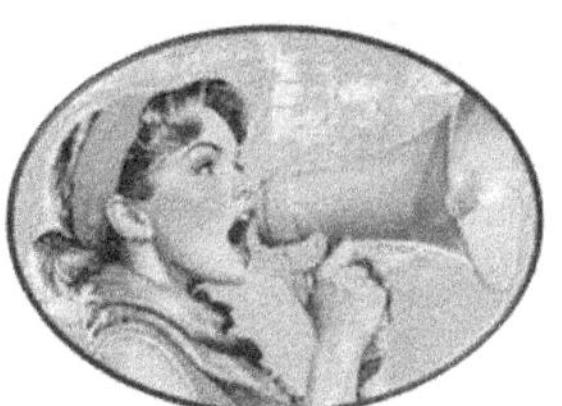

An aside here as I take a moment to step up on my soapbox:

Heaven-help-us-all, Honey, whatever you settle on, avoid those mall-produced-and-packaged glamour shots, long-armed-and-awkward selfies, phone-software-produced animal faces, or AI-generated memes. Just say NO. It just smacks of un-creativity, lack of professionalism, and, well, Ew.

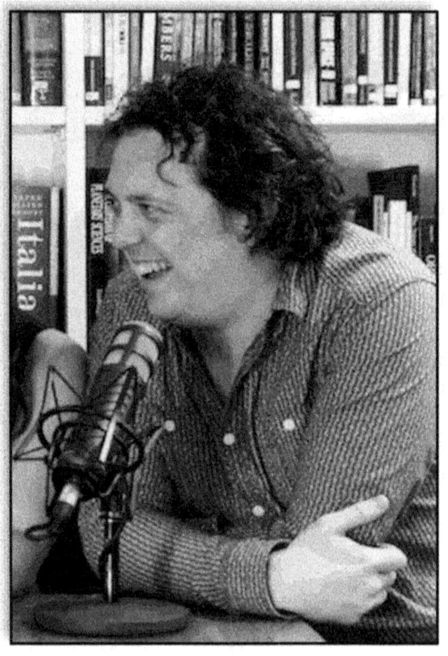
Italia

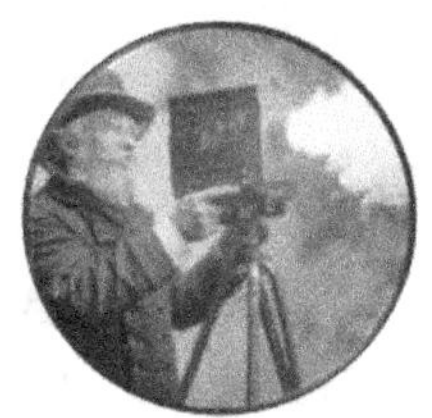

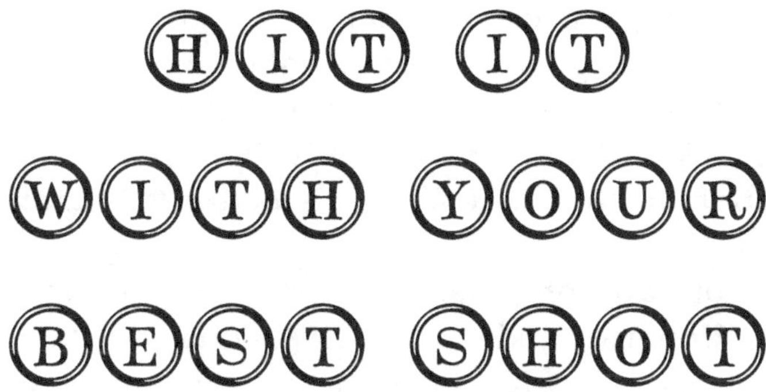

HIT IT WITH YOUR BEST SHOT

If budget allows, arrange for a session with a professional Photographer, as they will have high-quality equipment, backdrops, lighting, expertise, and experience, all worth paying for. Just be careful to select the Photographer carefully, someone who specializes in portraits, yet doesn't just pop out canned headshots.

Chat with several Photographers to be sure you find one who truly understands what you're after in Your Photo, and that they can deliver several options for you, in different outfits. Don't be afraid to show them examples of photos you feel deliver the look you seek.

Remember, this is an investment in your business, so don't be hesitant about the expense, you will use Your Photo for many years. And, yup, it is tax deductible.

On the day of the shoot, don't schedule anything else. You don't want to be stressed or in a hurry to get someplace. Also, be sure you're well-rested. Don't stay up late the night before, come zooming in from a red-eye flight, or show up sucking down energy drinks to recover from a night of... well, overindulgence, shall we call it? There is just not enough concealer in any makeup case for that. Every droopy bit of dull skin, saggy muscle, and dark circle and bag under your eyes will rear their ugliness in every shot and defeat the entire shoot. If you look in the mirror and don't recognize Your Persona looking back at you, ready for any challenge, then throw up your hands, Honey. It's better to surrender and reschedule.

Before any photo shoot you'll want to test out Your Persona Uniform and several versions by taking trial snapshots, seeing which deliver the best images of Your Persona. Resist an intentional "relaxed, casual" look that's too much, like a loose tie or open, floppy jacket. You could come off just looking sloppy or worse, *impaired.* Consult with others whose opinions you trust, too, to be sure Your Uniform conveys the story you wish to tell.

On the day of the shoot get dressed in your selected Persona Uniform, and plan to change into different ones during the shoot so you'll have choices later. Don't pick out anything that will take too long as you change outfits; your Photographer's time is money. Check to be sure your clothes don't look like they came from the bottom of the hamper. Starching and ironing pay off here. Keep jewelry simple.

Be sure you're looking good, like you're going out on a blind date with someone you really want to impress – because you are. Keep any hair and make-up unfussy and natural, yet neat and carefully done.

You may want to get your hair and makeup professionally done. If so, do it at least once beforehand to be sure it's the look you want, especially a new haircut or style. You don't want to show up for the shoot looking like a squirrel. Also, even if you think makeup isn't necessary, a bit of face powder will eliminate any distracting shiny spots on your face (or bald head).

If you put one foot slightly forward and twist your body slightly away from the lens, and sit or stand up straight, shoulders back, you'll look thinner. And who doesn't want that, I ask you...

Use the experienced model's trick to stand straight and look put-together: Plant yourself, then squeeze your butt. It'll lengthen your torso, drop your shoulders, push your hips forward, and tighten your stomach. Works wonders every time.

It's always nice to have a Photo Shoot Sidekick, someone you trust, at the shoot. Their only function is to stand in the background, studying you, so they can be on the lookout for fly-away hair or clothing malfunctions. They are also there to jump in with a quick reminder to pull your shoulders back. But be sure they understand who is in charge – and it is not them.

To produce a strong sense of connection in Your Photo, above all else, you want an engaged look in your eyes. Except for extremely moody shots, you'll want to be looking directly into the lens. You don't need to be smiling, but your eyes do. Yes, you want your eyes to smile. As the camera clicks, try looking at your Photo Shoot Sidekick and see if that cracks you up.

Take your time with everything.

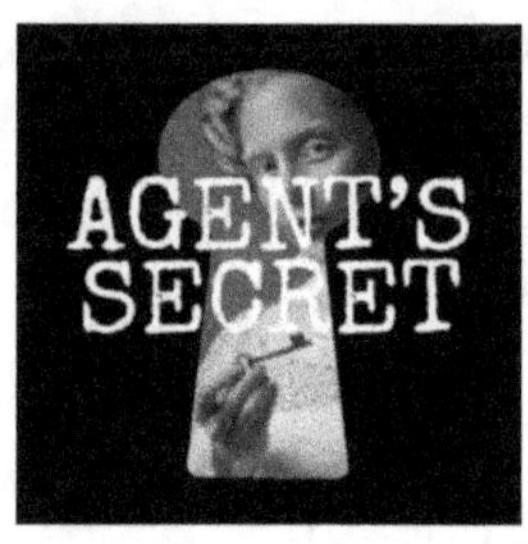

Want that gleam in your eyes?
Look directly at your lover.
Think of seducing someone. Anyone.
Conjure naughty thoughts.
Imagine ecstasy.
Now twinkle.

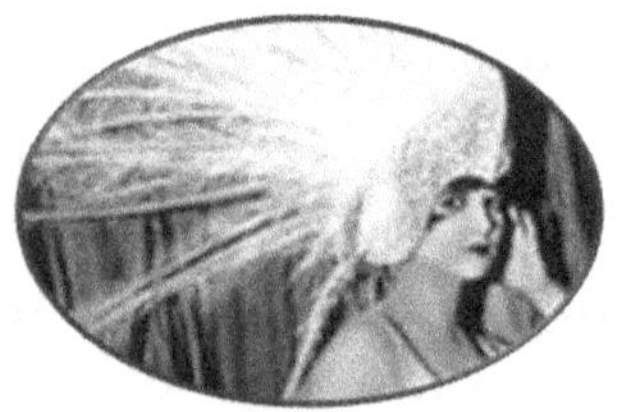

My 'Bama Gramma let it drop once that she knew a Ziegfeld Girl, a dancer from the famous Ziegfeld Follies on Broadway. Whispering to her, the Chorus Dancer revealed their very hush-hush technique to achieve that coveted, intriguing twinkle on stage. They wore silk panties from Paris.

&

CRICKET FREEMAN

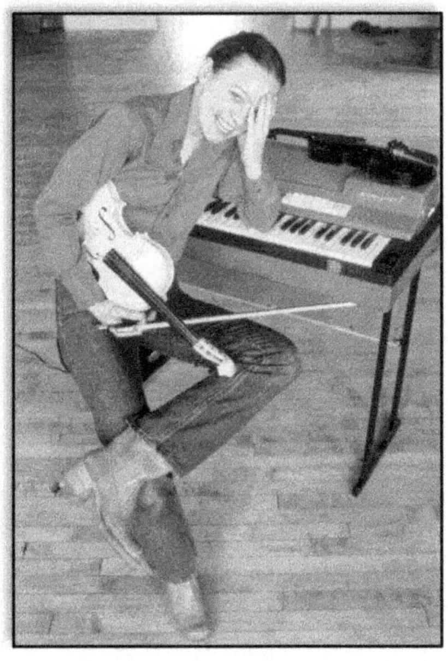

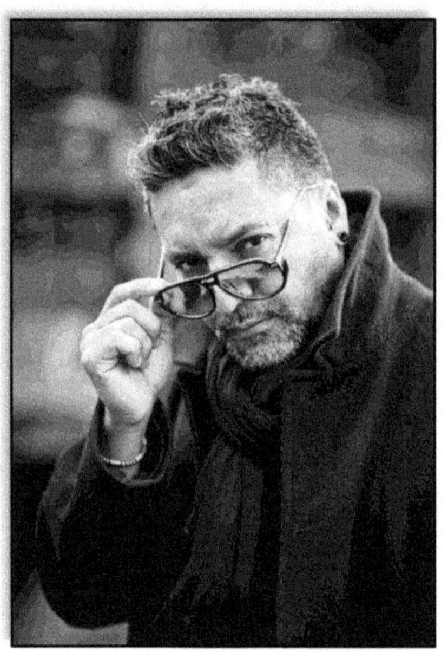

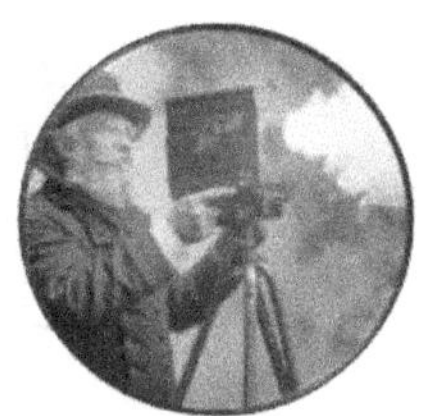

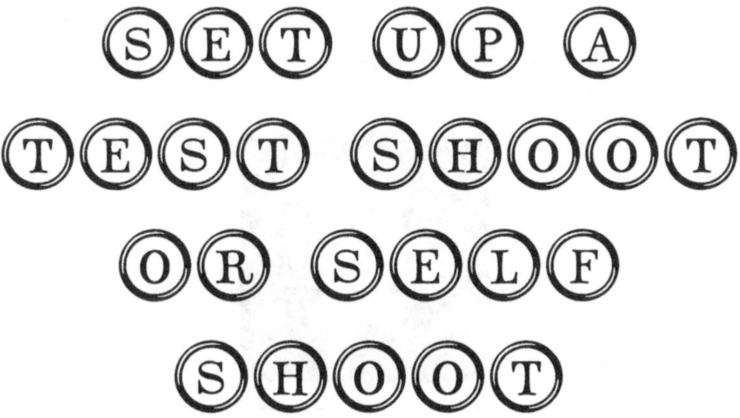

Stage a self shoot as a test prior to a professional photo shoot so you can supply your professional Photographer with your favorite poses, expressions, and outfits, and they can use their professional skills to upgrade your shots by recreating them under the best lighting and backgrounds.

But do you think you can use a quickie selfie as Your Photo, for everything? Don't even think about it, Honey. If you did it would be nothing short of self-sabotage. You work hard. You're passionate about your work. You deserve a fine photo to showcase that. What I am saying here is that, if you choose and have the skills, with time and care, a self shoot can produce a well-turned-out Photo that will work for many occasions, but not all.

All manner of new gizmos, doodads, and thingamabobs in tech – like computers, digital cameras, cell phone cameras, photo-editing software, portrait modes, auto focusing and lighting, phone holding clamps, cordless LED circle lights, levelling gimbals, and on and on – have made this process easy enough for most people to handle *if you're conscientious and you take the time.*

Here is but one reliable method for getting a solid Photo. Once you understand the process you might wish to try setting up a shoot on location.

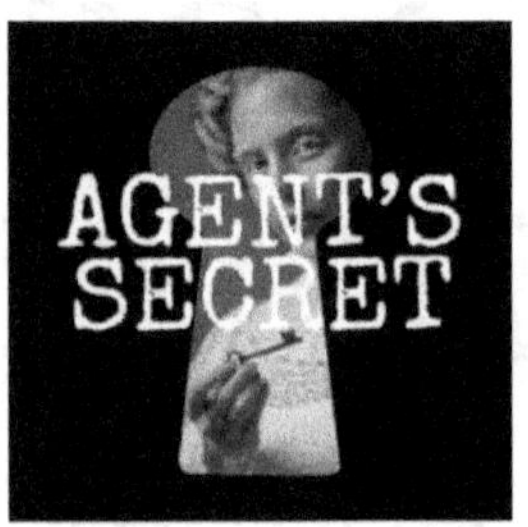

K eep
I t
S imple,
S tupid.

Gather the best equipment you can beg, borrow, or steal, Honey. (OK, that's an expression; don't take the last one seriously, unless it's from your annoying little brother and you'll get it back to him soon...) But, yes, you want to scope around and locate the best camera or camera phone with the best optics, plus tripods, lights, laptop with photo software, the works.

Gather up a friend or that above-mentioned annoying little brother to serve as your Photographer for your shoot.

If you can, also enlist the help of a Photo Shoot Sidekick to be a Photographer's Assistant, catching the little details you or the Photographer might miss. Older kids and teenagers can be surprisingly helpful as Photographers and Assistants. And you better take your crew for pizza afterwards. They will have earned it.

Plan on devoting an entire morning or afternoon to your shoot.

Use your dining room for your portrait studio, using a chair, table, and bright lamps.

Use contrast in your background; you don't want to blend in. If you have dark hair, then choose a light backdrop; if your hair is light, then a darker backdrop would be better.

To obtain a simple background in the shot that won't compete with your face, select a plain wall, either a solid wall with no pictures or woodwork visible, or a full set of solid drapes pulled closed. Also, you can try a solid tablecloth, sheet, or length of fabric as a draped background. Simply drape and clip it over a large picture, TV, drapery rod, bookshelf, door, or stair rail. You'd be surprised how good that can look.

Some of you may choose an old standby for your backdrop, such as bookshelves, ornate woodwork, or a brick wall. Photo backdrops are available for sale online for surprisingly little. Choose carefully. Simple is best.

Set a dining room chair or barstool in front of your chosen backdrop. Your Photographer might appreciate a chair or stool, too, to avoid rushing a shot.

Always use a tripod or one of those handy adjustable camera phone holders that clamp to a tabletop. Lacking a tripod or holder, simply set the camera or phone up on a stack of books on the table and for stability, nestle it onto the top of a bag of rice or beans.

Turn on every light in the room, adding some extra lamps on surrounding tables or use pole lamps or clamp-type lamps at shoulder-height on bookshelves, cabinet doors, or drapery rods. You can try light from windows, but it can be harsh, not very controllable, and difficult to balance. The more lights you have, from more directions, the fewer ornery shadows you'll have. However, avoid any from behind or directly overhead. Never have lights shining up from below – you'll look like a silent-film ghoul from a zombie movie.

Be sure the light is shining on your face and is coming from both the left and right to eliminate any unfortunate shadows on your face or behind you.

Have your Photographer frame the shot. Sometimes the best shot is taken from farther away, using the zoom to frame you in the shot, thus fuzzing the background. Note, however, that some digital cameras reduce the number of pixels as you zoom, so sharpness might deteriorate if you want to blow up the finished photo.

Use your Photographer's Assistant as your stand-in and check what the camera sees. Check the lighting, the drape of the background, any shadows, and the composition of the shot.

Now sit in the chair and gather your composure for the shoot. Have your Photographer's Assistant assure that your hair is fine, with no outlaw strands, and all looks good.

Take a few test shots, trying some shots with a flash, on auto flash, and with turning off the flash on the camera.

Now review all the shots together, using a laptop if you can, so you can see the photos on a larger screen. Check to be sure the lighting, framing, and background are what you're after. Make any needed adjustments. The more shots you take, the wider your choices will be. No need to be stingy with digital; all shots are free. The only cost here is time.

Push your creativity, using different lighting and as many different poses, expressions, and gestures, as you can conjure up. Sometimes the craziest ends up being the best.

Stand up, sit on something, lean against anything.

Lean forward, lean back, turn left, turn right, full front view, ¾ view.

Sit up straight, slump, twist to one side.

Put your chin in your hand, clasp your hands under your chin, cock your head.

Take off your glasses, wear your glasses, hold your glasses, wear sunglasses.

Turn the chair around and straddle it, put your arms on the chair back.

Turn your back to the camera and look over your shoulder, use your hands and arms.

Look playful, questioning, forceful, intent, reflective, intrigued, shy, sexy, or commanding – any emotions you wish to project as Your Persona.

Forget the Photographer; get lost watching TV, reading, or listening to the Assistant read aloud.

Have your Photographer or Photo Shoot Sidekick remind you of memories, people, and subjects to solicit a variety of emotions and expressions, like, "Think of how you felt holding your baby for the first time," "...the time you saw your first crush across the room at a school dance," "...the first time you hit a homerun," "...the first time your saw your spouse naked." You get the idea. Have fun. Make jokes. Laugh a lot.

Take your time with everything. Calming music helps slow everyone down.

Take LOTS of photos.

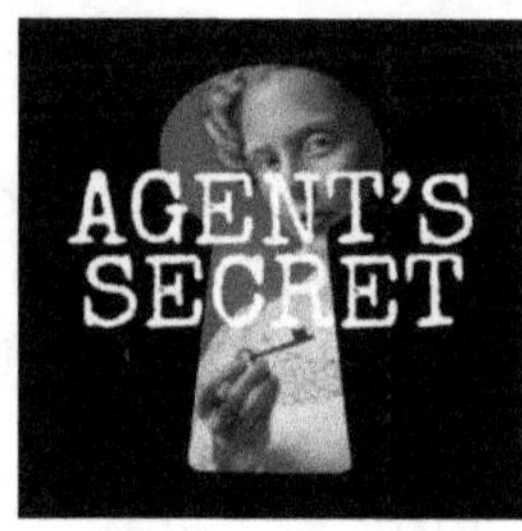

Position the camera above eye level.
Imagine a cord pulling your head up.
Turn your head a little to the side.
Lift your chin ever-so-slightly.
Look straight at the top of the lens.
Now twinkle.

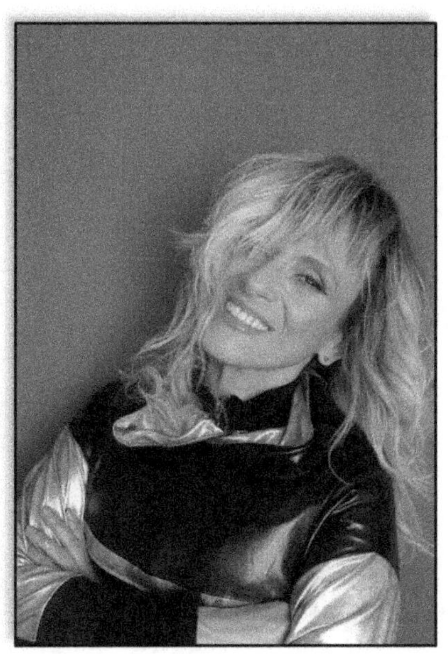

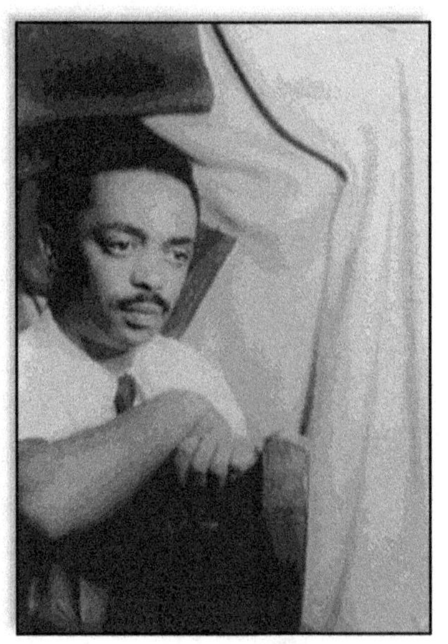

> *"The true portrait of a man is a fusion of what he thinks he is, what others think he is, what he really is, and what he tries to be."*
>
> *~ Dore Schary*

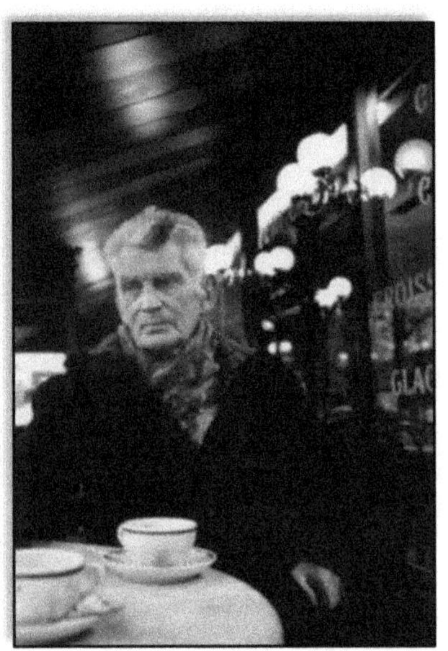

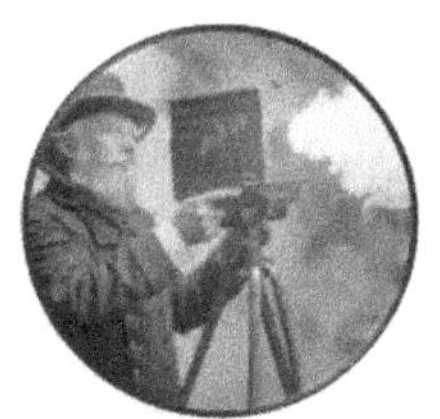

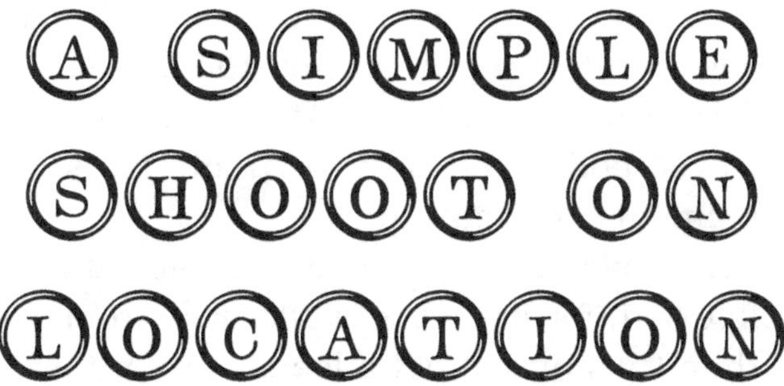

A SIMPLE SHOOT ON LOCATION

When it comes to backgrounds, certainly think outside the box. Putting you in an intriguing setting makes you intriguing. You and your Photographer may decide a location will give you a background to deliver more of your story, bring more emotion to Your Photo, and better connect with your Readers, Listeners, or Viewers. But keep in mind, a professional Photographer may charge extra for travel, so take that into consideration. However, it might be an expense you're willing to make for results.

Anywhere in nature is advantageous for Your Photo, so consider, for example:

- At the beach. It's inviting and cosmically connecting.
- In the woods. Varied foliage provides texture and interest.
- On the water. Any lake, river, or ocean provides a sensuous background.

- In, on, or next to a car, boat, motorcycle, horse, jet ski, camel, or plane. It should relate to your work, such as on a battleship or tank for a military Reporter. It beckons the viewer to go where you lead.
- In an exotic locale. A ski slope, a botanical garden, or even the neighborhood hardware store might offer up exactly what you seek. But remember, you want intriguing, not ludicrous. Laughing, arms up on a roller coaster, might work well for a travel podcaster, but turn off Fans if you're a political commentator.
- On a road or path. Again, "Come with me." Add a flourish, for instance, walk away from the camera, then turn and shoot a look over your shoulder.
- In front of famous landmarks. It's another version of "Come with me." Be sure it relates to the subject of your work, though, such as the Golden Gate Bridge for a travel Host, or Sax Fifth Avenue for a fashion Influencer.
- In front of architectural detailing. It works well as a background, especially an intricate doorway, which suggests entering your world, like in a Victorian entry for a historical Novelist or a history Podcaster.
- Deep in weather. Snow, wind, even rain can add a fabulous evocative layer to your Photo. Is it any wonder Photographers turn on electric Fans for great model shots?

- Using props. Easy does it, though. Overdo it at your foolish peril. However, sometimes, a simple addition can tell a story, adding emotion, like cradling a bowl in a chef YouTuber's hand, even holding a gun for a thriller Novelist, but make sure your chosen prop is secondary to you. Note: Never have a drink in your hand; that will backfire on you, no matter what your intention.

Wherever you go on location, remember you are outside. Move, and capture that action in your Photo to bag even more emotion and connection.

Pay attention to the lighting outside, it can be tricky – and changeable. Some Photographers use reflective sunscreens (yup, like the ones you use in your windshield to keep your car cool during the Summer) to bounce the light up onto your face.

For the most flattering light, choose early mornings or late afternoons.

Avoid the harsh light of high noon.

Cloudy days can produce soft, subtle lighting.

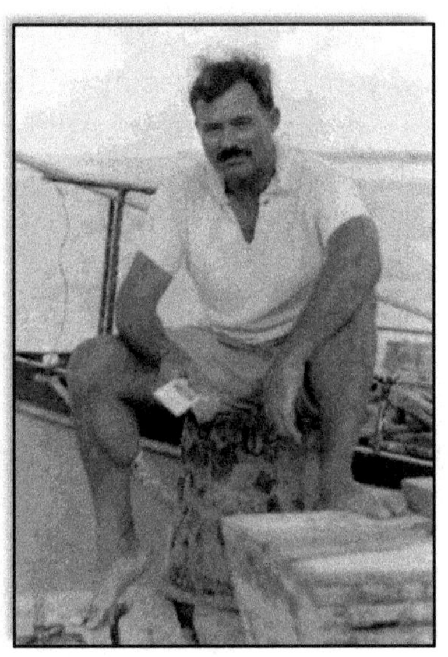

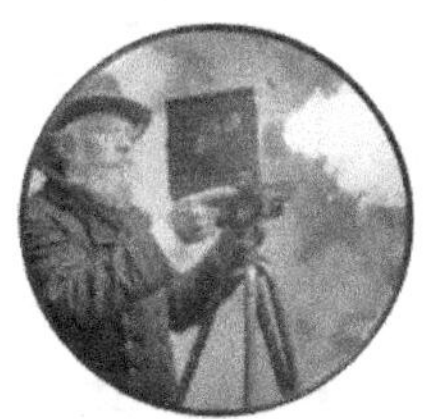

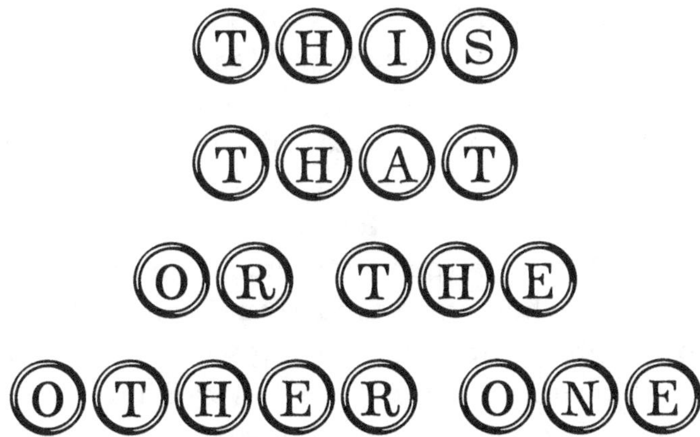

After downloading all your photos to a computer, you now have time to review and manipulate them. Don't shortchange yourself here. You can make or break Your Photo in this part of the process.

Print test shots of each photo in color and black and white so you can peruse them thoroughly. You'd be staggered by what emerges sometimes that you can only see once it's in print. Many photos will look amazing only in black and white, and iffy in color. Or the reverse may be true. So, there's your first sorting criteria.

Next, select only photos that are in keeping with projecting Your Persona to your target audience so they can connect with you.

Now, sort the photos into three groups: The Keepers, the Possibilities, and the Never-Evers. You'll spot the Keepers right away, they're awesome.

The Never-Evers smack you pretty quickly, too. These are the ones you can eliminate that have poor lighting, reflections, contrast, clarity, composition, odd clothing issues, stupid looks, closed eyes, or goofy expressions, like you just smelled something you wish you hadn't.

The majority, most likely, will fall into the Possibilities, ones that could work, if you or your Photographer take the time to edit them in a photo-editing software, such as Photoshop.

Concentrate on the Keepers group to produce your best Photo. Crop, sharpen, darken, brighten, or soften as needed. This is where you'll find Your Photo.

You might want to try playing with any photos in the Possibilities group, and even the Never-Evers, to see what extra you can discover. But don't spend too much time with them; you have your Keepers.

For instance, I've mined the mess of Possibilities and Never Evers and found golden gifts. Start by cropping out any extraneous, distracting elements. Zero in on your face. Try unusual, asymmetric crops for an artistic shot, such as getting so close-in that you crop off the top of your head or only show one eye. These tightly-cropped photos can be unexpected and wonderful, extremely useful as online icons.

If you or your Photographer are good in your photo-editing software, there's very little you can't do, from removing dark circles under your eyes, removing a mole, or whitening your teeth. However, just be sure in the final product, you do look like you. Nothing screams "*AMATEUR!*" like an overworked photo.

Save all photos in a common format, such as jpeg, (B&W and color) so they can be easily posted, texted, emailed, and generally shared and used by everyone else down the line. Be sure to save in different resolutions as you'll need at least 300-600 dpi for print media, and any more than 96 dpi for the web usually takes longer than necessary to load, even with high-speed internet.

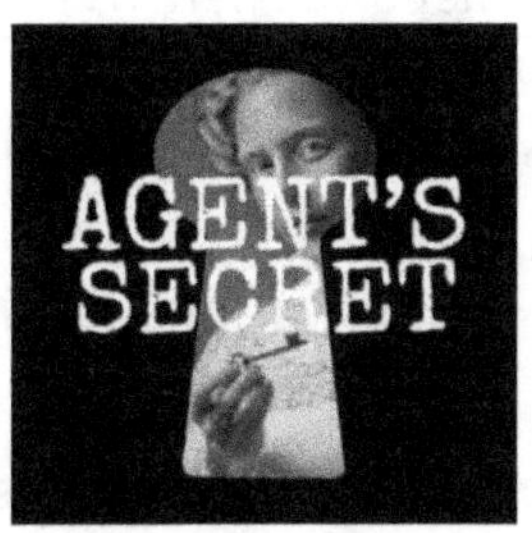

Your Photo holds up a mirror for Fans.
You decide the Persona they see.
Denote professional.
Reveal intriguing.
Display calm and confident.

Nothing says success like confidence.

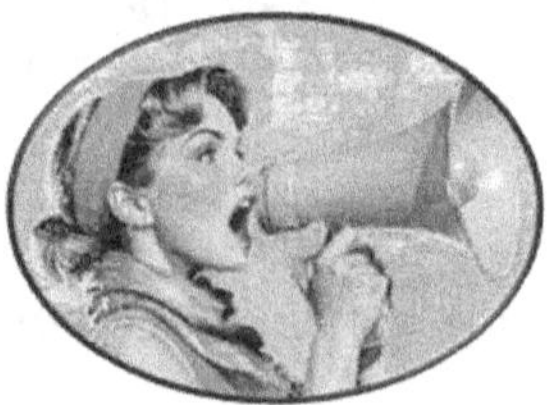

Another aside here as I climb up on my soapbox again:

When it comes to Your Photo, avoid AI like the plague, Honey.

I know, I know, it's amazing, and can do so many things. True. You may think it's grand, but none of us have any idea how AI may rudely pop up in the future to sabotage you, following some digital footprints, and somehow, brand you a Big, Fat Faker.

For now, old school is safe school.

CRICKET FREEMAN

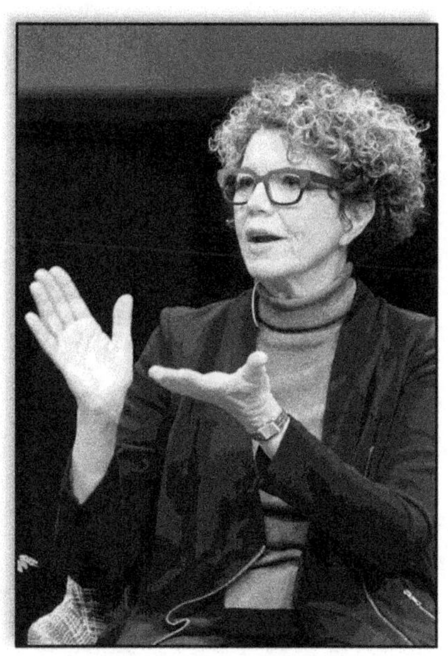

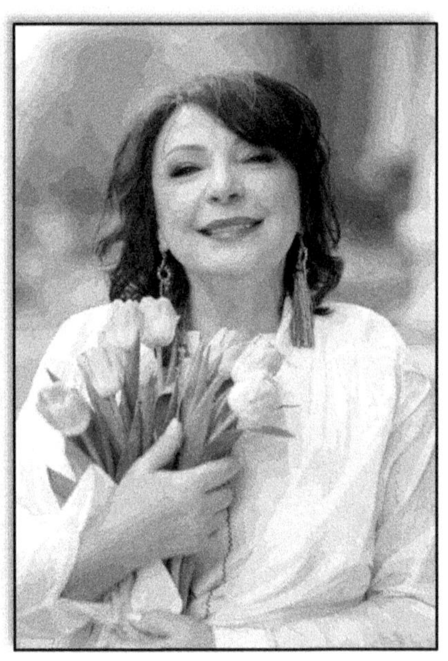

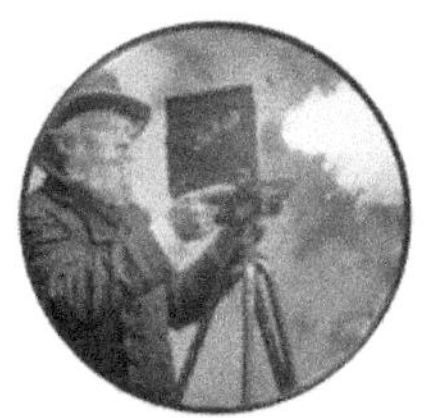

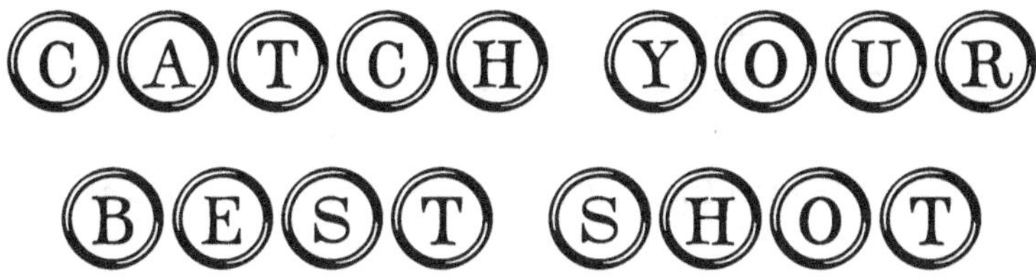

- [ ] Are you foremost in Your Photo? Or are you lost in the background or surroundings?
- [ ] What feeling does Your Photo convey?
- [ ] Does it reflect Your Persona?
- [ ] Does Your Photo show Your Persona as a real, live, breathing, feeling, authentic person? Or does it look like a nameless, brainless model or film character grinning from a cheesy, cheap picture frame?
- [ ] Does Your Photo capture the emotion your Fans crave?
- [ ] Do your eyes grab and hold the viewer, imploring them to connect with you?
- [ ] Do you look like you've been captured in the middle of doing something – something important (and, yes, that includes thinking)? Or do you look artificially posed?

- ☐ Does Your Uniform represent your Persona in a genuine and realistic way?
- ☐ Have you used the background, lighting, and any props to your advantage?
- ☐ Does the location mean something to your Fans?
- ☐ Is Your Photo technically of good quality for reproduction?
- ☐ Is it well-balanced, with good composition?
- ☐ Is there good contrast?
- ☐ Is it free of distracting elements, such as awkward shadows?
- ☐ Does Your Photo look equally well in color and in black & white?
- ☐ Can Your Photo be cropped for an alternate Photo, one more artistic, hip, or with a fresh attitude?
- ☐ Do you have several photos available for various uses and platforms?
- ☐ Does Your Photo leave your potential audience thirsting, "I want some of *THAT* – and I'm willing to spend time and money for it."?

&

CRICKET FREEMAN

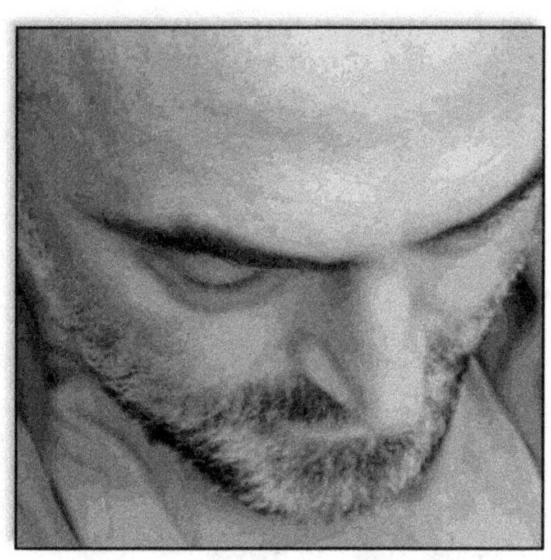

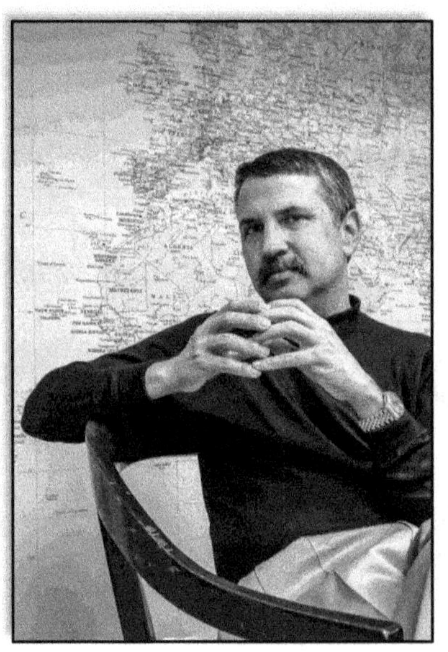

"There is nothing worse than a brilliant image of a fuzzy concept."

~ Ansel Adams

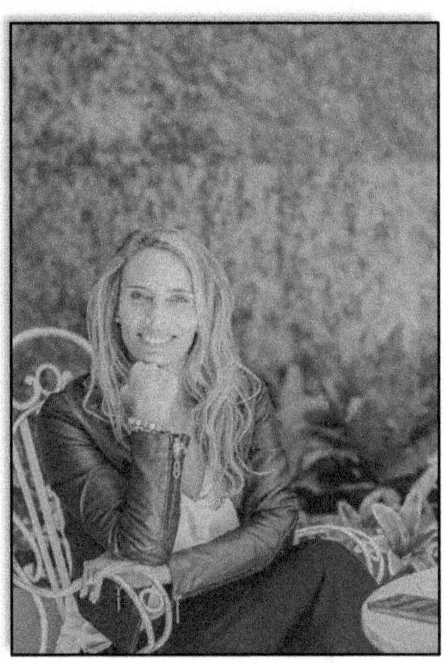

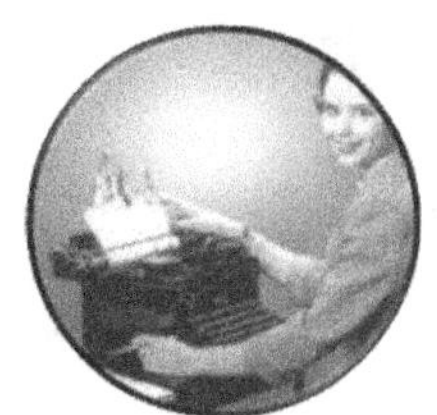

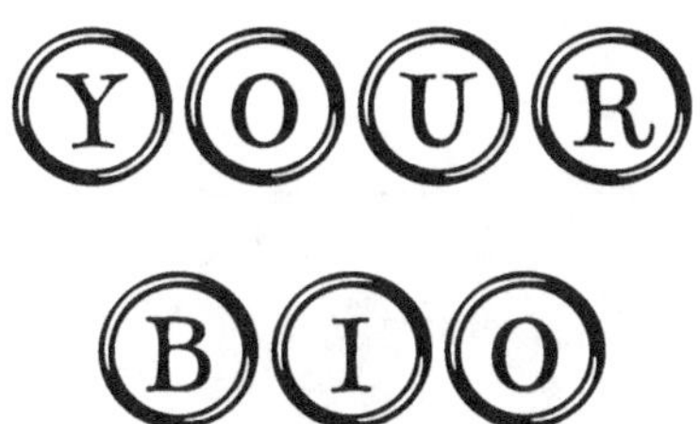
YOUR
BIO

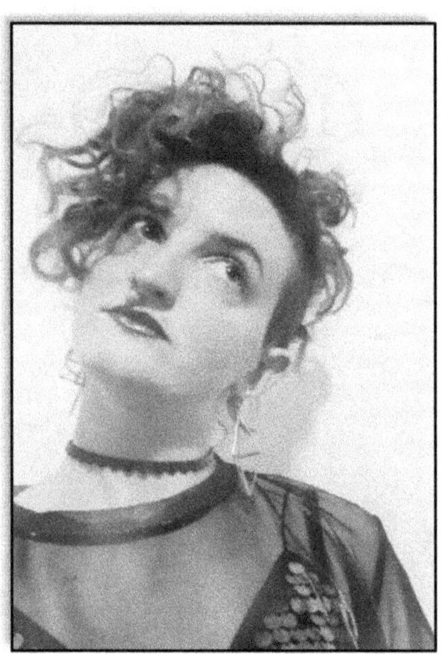

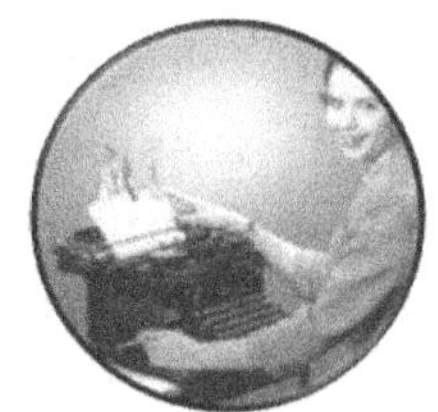

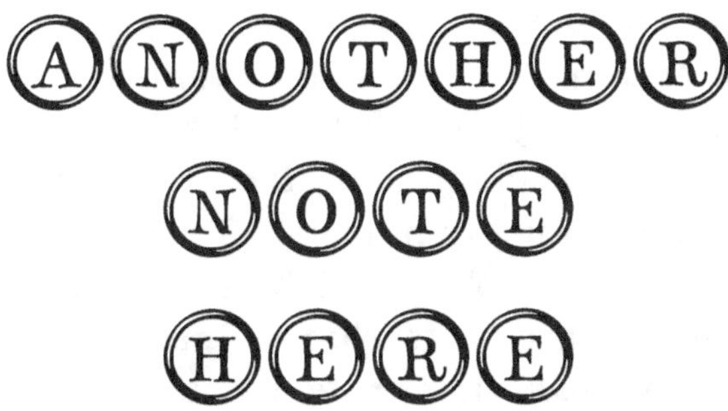

Here's how it is from someone who's been there, done that, and looked at thousands of Photos and Bios, making decisions that could impact or shake up those people from that point forward. And, no, I never took the responsibility blithely – because I knew how those people felt. I was often on the flip side of the desk myself, having someone else make a high-speed decision about me and my work based on a Photo and a Bio.

For an example of just how crucial Your Photo and Bio are, let me tell you about a submission package that came to my literary agency years ago. A sample of the writing pulled me in, lots do that, but it was more than that. John's Photo and Bio were so well done I was beyond intrigued. I was impressed. To be more accurate, I was flat out at a standstill until I knew more about him, about his work.

His Photo and Bio showed me he was knowledgeable and passionate about his work, and more than that, a professional who could make things happen. He had my attention full tilt and now I needed to connect with him. I was hooked. But somehow his contact info just wasn't there. I rummaged and rifled through my desk, old emails, the trash can, everywhere I could think to dig. All I could find was his name and the name of a town. Nothing else.

I tried to drop it, but his Photo and Bio wouldn't let go of me, his eyes drilling into me from his Photo, remembering bits from his Bio, keeping me on the phone off-and-on for a couple of days, tracking him down. (Today, with Google and other magic, I'd probably ferret him out within an hour.) Luckily, by jumping clue to clue, I finally reached a fabric shop in the small town that knew his mom, they had her call me, and within a few minutes my phone rang. It was him. I squealed like a little girl.

I've often thought about that ragged introduction to a new talent. If I didn't have such a dynamic Photo and Bio to snag me, I never would have been drawn in, and I certainly wouldn't have been so driven as to track him down. I'd have gone on to the next project on my desk nagging for attention.

Your Photo and Bio can generate that same power so that your Readers, Listeners, and Viewers will seek out your work, writing, posts, videos, and become your Fans. And today you can connect easily and safely by including a call to action, a link to your social media and your website.

Your Photo can generate the power to grab them, but it is Your Bio that can generate the power to draw them in deeper. And that's simply because you have more room to express yourself and connect with them, giving them what they're looking for, something that will excite and intrigue them. Something to hook them, just as I was.

Maybe it's something they don't even know they want yet.

As an Editor I learned that the success of any project depends on delivering to your target audience all their desires, needs, longings, curiosities, snoopings, and wishes, like a Genie in a Bottle. Your Bio is that Genie.

However, I also learned – often the hard way, I might add – to keep in mind the doubts, debacles, anxieties, reservations, pinches, conundrums, and boring bits that could pop up to bite you in your backside if you're not careful and unknowingly drop something useless or glitchy into Your Bio. I know, because I've run smack dab up against them, too, for decades.

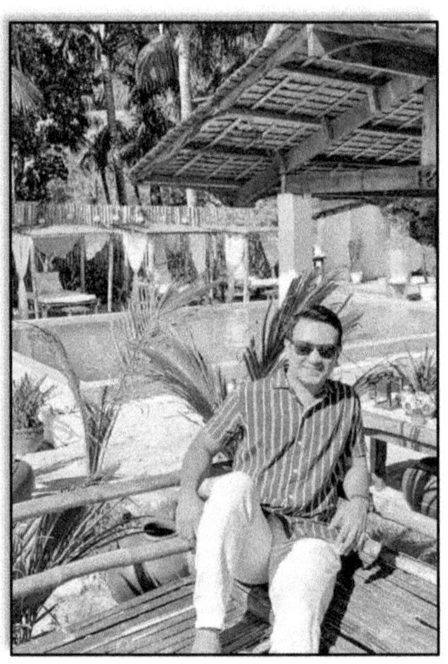

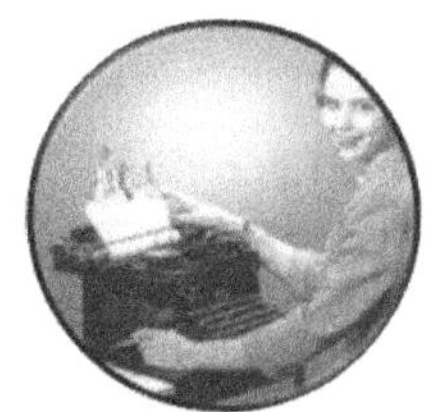

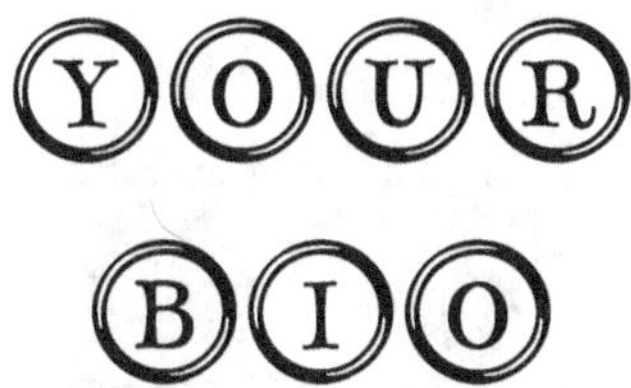

YOUR BIO

You absolutely need a super Bio because it is the most effective marketing tool you have, along with Your Photo, to market Your Persona so that you can market your work. But not just any Bio will do. You need something that will deliver more than dry information, something more than a paragraph or two which gets quickly scanned and tossed aside without another thought.

You need something to catch the eye of Viewers, Readers, Listeners, but also to supply focus, reflect who you are, spark interest, make you memorable, present your perspective. To make that oh-so-desired connection.

However, Your Bio also needs to build a brand name, create a buzz, and push past your competition.

All that may be a lot, and you say you have it under control, right? Writing your own Bio is easy. After all, you already know all there is to know. No studying required.

But don't get ahead of your know-it-all self. That's just the problem, Sweet Cheeks, you know *TOO* damn much.

So how do you fire up Your Bio to red-hot? How can you possibly sift through all of what you know to narrow it down to exactly the right details to make you stand out in a crowded marketplace of thousands, all competing for those same eyes?

With purpose and precision.

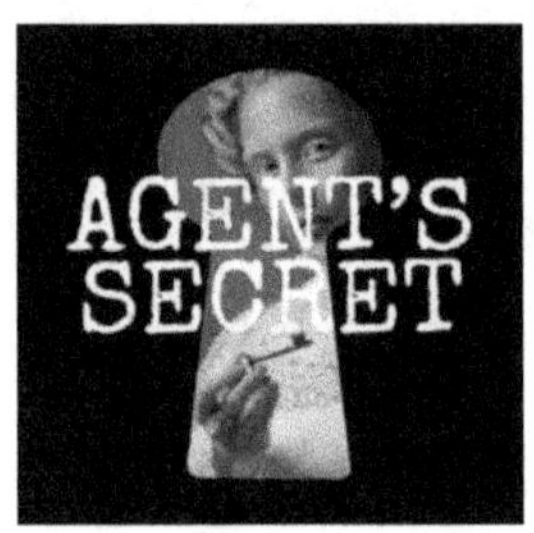

> Writing a good Bio is akin to bonsai.
> The trick is to know what to prune.
> Yet leave an artful idea of the whole.
> It's an interpretation of Your Persona.

You want to make Your Persona – through Your Bio – fascinating, informed, charming, wise, captivating, alluring, compelling, fun, authoritative, and intriguing.

You want to be all these things because a Bio is designed for one purpose, and only one purpose: to attract Readers, Listeners, and Viewers pondering whether to drop twenty bucks or twenty minutes on what *YOU* have to say.

Give them something to make them believe you're worth taking the risk.

But Your Bio is not your autobiography, nor a list of facts or greatest hits. Neither are you writing your obituary. And your dating-site-*de-jour* listing? Oh, my.... Yes, I've seen Bios that sounded like each of those things.

On the other hand, breaking everything down like this just to produce a few sentences for Your Bio may sound daunting to you, even impossible. Some people feel writing their Bio is the toughest backbreaker they've ever attempted. They just can't get there from here. Doing what they do? Easy. Writing their own Bio? A conundrum.

I suppose they're just way too close to the subject to get objective, much less entertaining. And their heads are just too full of the hodgepodge and jumble of their life to whittle it all down to a paragraph or two. Or, it could be, I suppose, they could be just too damn lazy to care about taking the time and effort needed to produce an effective Bio. But that's not you, is it?

Imagine you're going to be a guest on a morning news show. What would you want to hear announced as you wait to waltz out and join the host on camera? Lots of cool stuff. OK, write that down. It'll give you something to work with, something to build upon. Of course, you don't want to end up with an exaggerated puff piece or to fib about who you are, just paint Your Persona in the best light.

Now, if you're a virginal first-timer, just dipping your toe in the water, don't worry you're too inexperienced with no credentials. You just need to sound compelling.

One writers' group I met had a cool solution to the Bio-writing challenge. When Maggie found herself looking down the throat of writing her bio, she gasped, folded, and threw up her hands in overwhelmed surrender. Her critique group came riding in on white horses. They pulled out all those fascinating little details that made her a very real person, and each one wrote their version of a snazzy Bio. She ended up with a selection of lengths, styles, voices, and tasty phrases, and the confidence to whip it all into a dynamic Author's Bio.

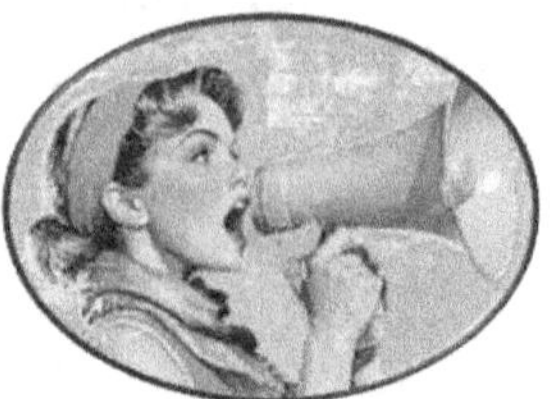

This time I have to hop up on my soapbox because I feel compelled to save you from yourself.

Whatever you do, and no matter how hard you're tempted, don't you dare cough up a Bio that's a dry, gagging grocery list of dates and schools you attended, towns you've lived in, how you aced the third grade spelling bee, why you took pen to paper at the ripe old age of three, found your true self on stage, or jumped in front of a mike in high school. Blah, blah, blah.

Readers, Viewers, Listeners want more than that and you owe it to them. And certainly never, ever, ever start out with some snore fest like, "Suzy was born in 1997 in Minot, North Dakota..." You'll have them falling face down in their oatmeal.

And, now again, a word about AI:

If you decide to turn to the latest tool (or sham, depending on your viewpoint) to do it for you, you may be happy, you may not. Just be sure Your Persona is accurately portrayed. Be sure Your Bio is authentic.

Absolutely, you want to avoid the mundane, the typical, the clichéd, the corny, and the cheesy. Who wants to squander their time on that crap? These days no one can afford wasted time blown to the four winds. They just click on – or swipe left. Don't you?

Instead, make it your duty to grab their flitting attention and lock it down. Show some attitude. Turn up the juice. Make this a showpiece to introduce Viewers, Listeners, Readers to Your Persona. Use your glorious gift of gab to tell a story and hook them as Fans.

What this means is that you leave out the snoozers, like "Joe was born in Cleveland." and "She graduated from M.I.T." Instead, you, the fascinating Persona, write: "Rock 'n roll flowed through Joe's veins long before the Hall of Fame struck its first chord in his hometown." or "Her chemistry degree from M.I.T. distinguished her in the world of professional cooking and characterized her unpredictable recipes."

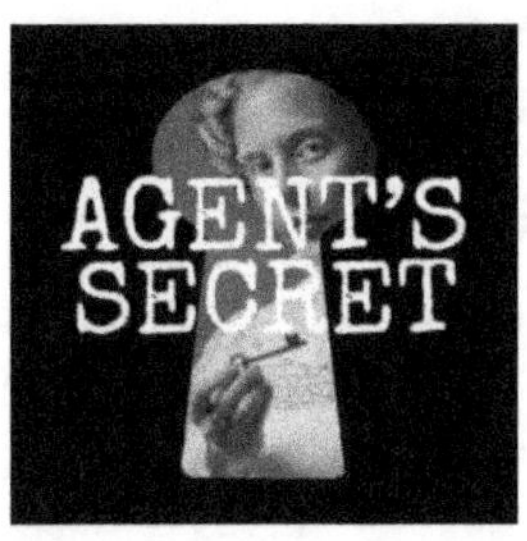

Fans want to know YOU.

Not what you've DONE.

They want to know WHO YOU ARE.

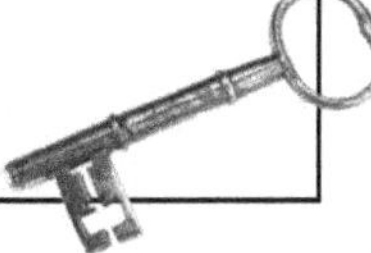

OK, time for tough talk. You want Readers, Listeners, and Viewers to give you a *GOOD* look, and stick around long enough to connect, right? Well, then, you need to double down and *REALLY* look at yourself, in detail, to give them the niceties and fine points they need to connect with.

Your Persona needs to connect with them so they can connect with you.

So, let's begin by breaking it down into Who, Where, What, Why, When, and How.

"Life is like a grapefruit. It's sort of orangey-yellow and dimpled on the outside, wet and squidgy in the middle. It's got pips inside, too. Oh, and some people have half a one for breakfast."

~ Douglas Adams

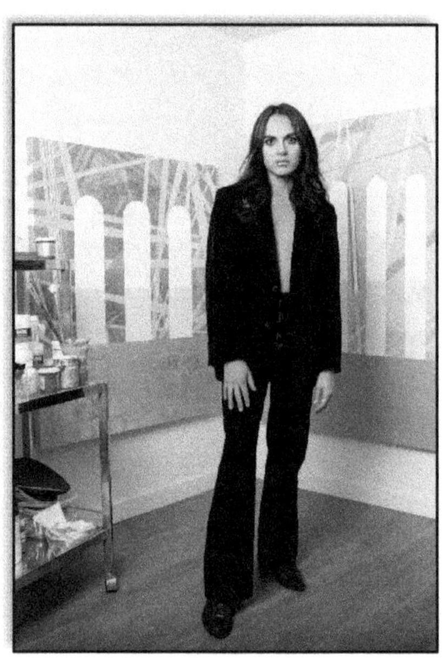

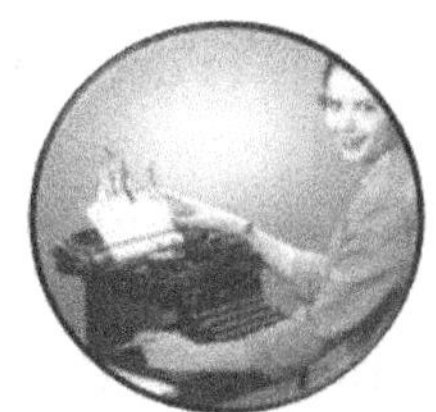

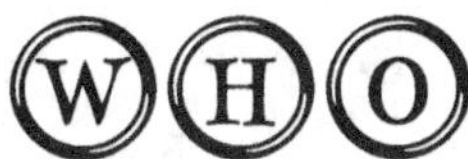

Your Persona, your brand, your work, needs to escape being lumped in with all your competition vying for your audience at any given moment. You need to rise above the thousands of rather-acceptable, but-mundane, nothing-out-of-the-ordinary, oh-so-numbingly-boringly-plain-vanilla, and therefore unspectacular-and-unremarkable others out there. You're better than that, aren't you? You bet your Jolly Ranchers you are.

But what is it that could set your apart, that makes some people hotter properties than others?

Hot properties stand out. Consider, though, there are lots of ways of standing out. What we're talking about here is to be sure Your Persona stands out like a spectacular Cinderella at the Ball. Not a raging Hulk on a rooftop. Or worse, like a stinking trout on a table. You know what I'm talking about here. We've all seen the Hulks, and the trouts – and groaned.

You certainly want Your Persona to stand out in a crowded marketplace, but without looking amateurish, desperate, or ridiculous.

Your Persona that you develop is exactly what defines and sets you apart from the competition. It is the True You. It is what makes you unique.

And always keep in mind: Your most passionate champion will always be You.

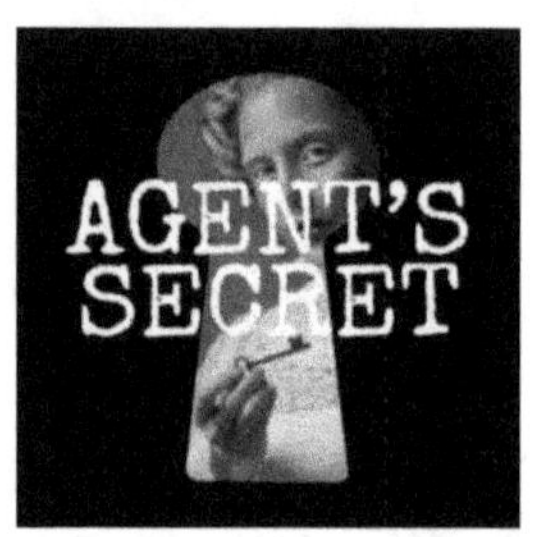

Being authentic is catnip to Fans.

Being unique sells.

> *"Styles, like everything else, change. Style does not."*
>
> *~ Linda Ellerbee*

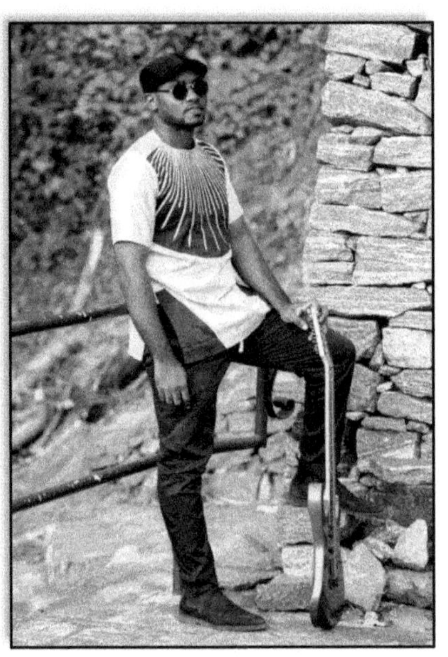

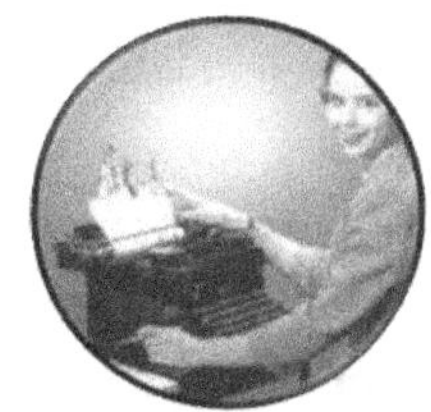

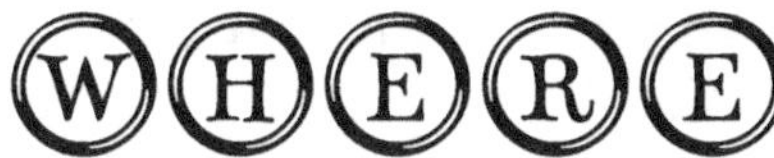

Versions of Your Photo and Bio will land in any number of places from social media sites, video sites, in online searches, in the press, on streaming services, you name it. That's how it goes today. Anywhere, everywhere. In a blink.

However, the primary place you will utilize Your Photo and Your Bio is on your own website. You have all the control here so you can present Your Persona in full spotlight. You can post several Photos in full color, however you like, and Your Bio can be as involved as you choose with no restraints on word count. Glorious. With a good one, your Readers, Viewers, or Listeners will have no excuse not to spend time getting to know you, to appreciate your work.

You can post samples of your previous works and extras, such as interviews, reviews, links to similar sites, recommendations, games, quizzes, even calls to action, such as signing up for a newsletter.

The main objective is for you to collect contact information when your Fans visit your website so that you can maintain a data base for keeping in touch with them. Vital.

Think of it as your mothership, so no matter what other social media you use, places where your Fans hang out, you will want to lead your Fans to your own website.

Remember to keep your website changing and dynamic so Fans will return often, seeking something new.

Your website is your mothership because your own website is the spot where you have ultimate control and this is where you can make the most lucrative opportunities to monetize your Fans.

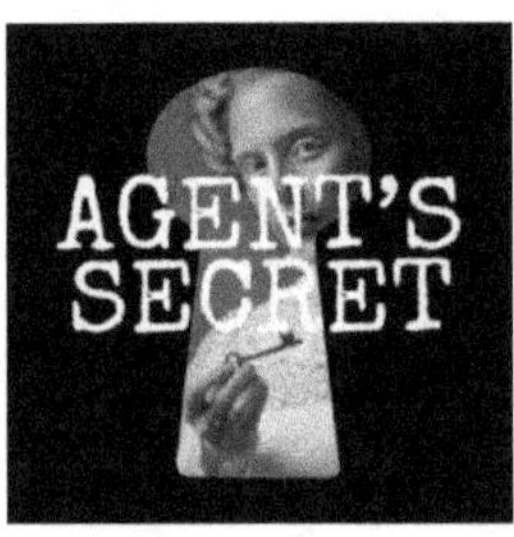

Feed your fans.

In turn, they will feed you.

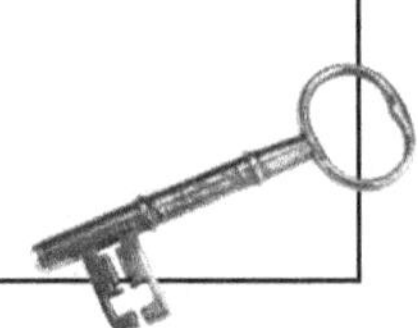

&

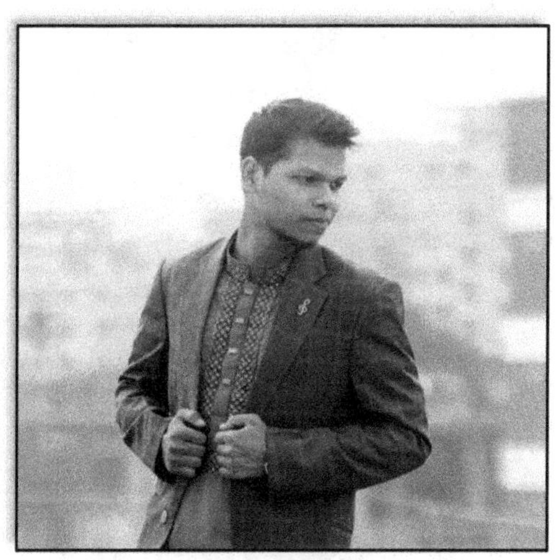

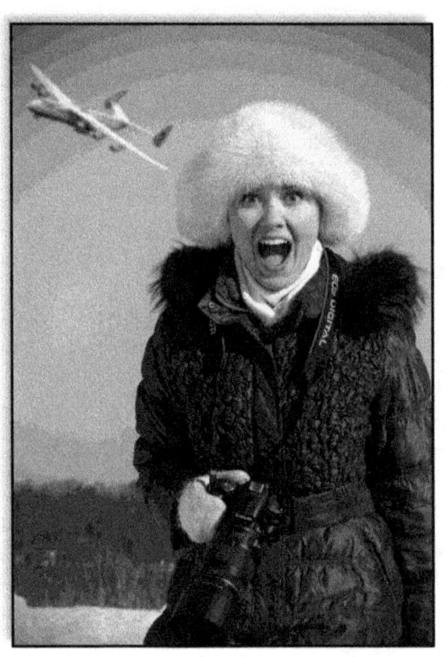

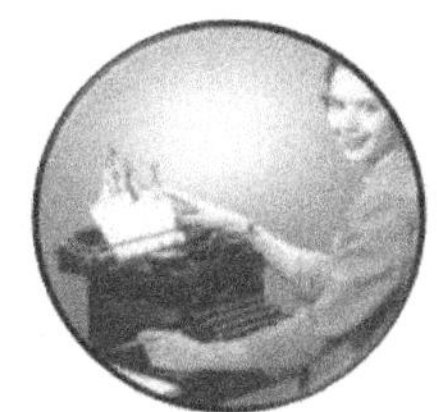

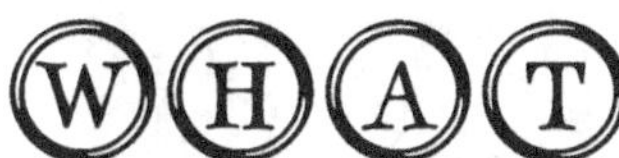

When you're asking Readers, Viewers, and Listeners to gamble their time with you, you should do all you can in Your Bio to offer up lots of points of possible connection between Your Persona and your Fans. Lots of humanity, lots of emotion, lots of feel good. Lots of juicy, relatable detail.

Your Bio should also instill confidence and cultivate goodwill, while showing that you are a distinctive professional. One who is worth their time. One who is willing, able, and oh-so-ready to deliver exactly what they are looking for. To be their Genie in a Bottle, granting all their wishes. And you're all about that, aren't you?

So, now, then, think about this: Have you ever gone into a bakery, ordered a dozen donuts, and when you reached for your favorite raised and glazed found thirteen donuts instead? Did it put a smile on your face? I know it did. Called a baker's dozen by most people, it's that little bit of something extra, what Louisiana Cajuns call a lagniappe. We don't expect it, but, *damn*, we all love it. Why? Because it shows a generosity of spirit, a willingness to do more than expected, without expecting anything extra in return.

If you give your Listeners, Readers, or Viewers more in Your Bio than the dull drivel they've come to expect, then you're delivering that beloved baker's dozen. You will make them smile.

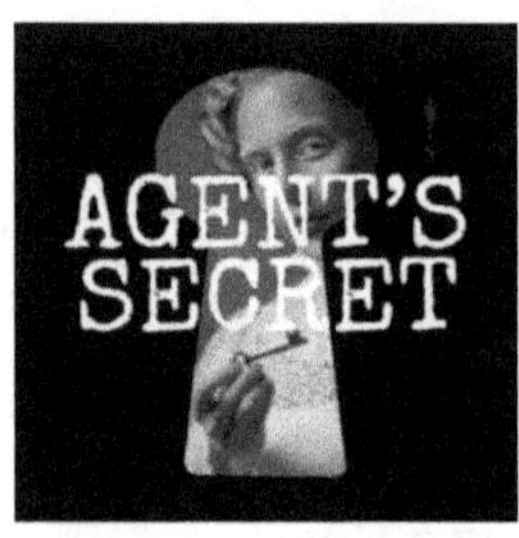

Deliver the unexpected: MORE.

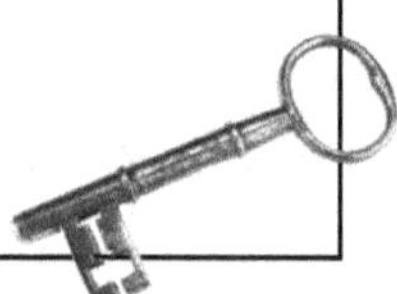

CRICKET FREEMAN

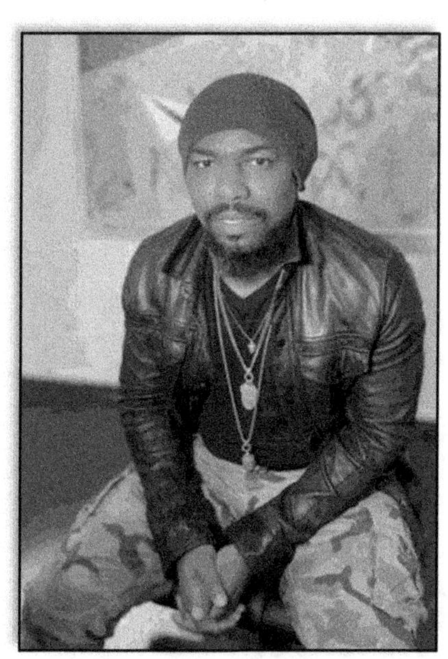

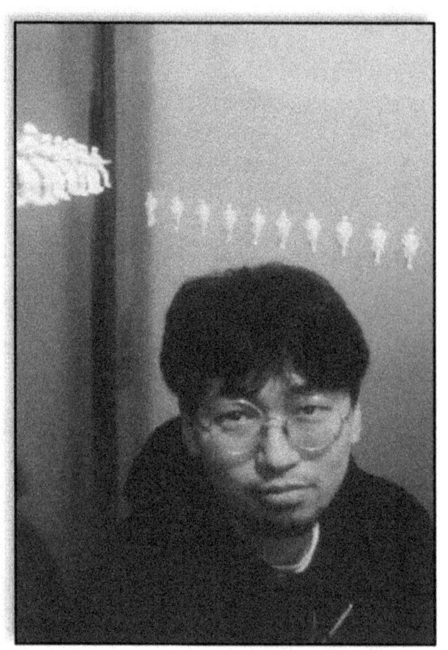

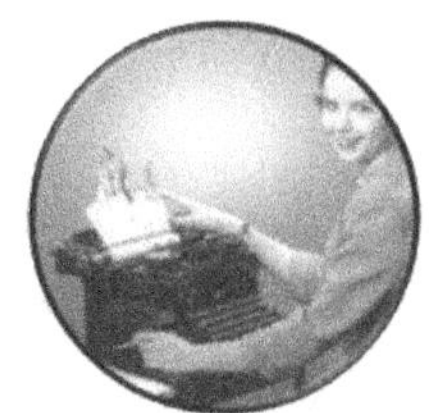

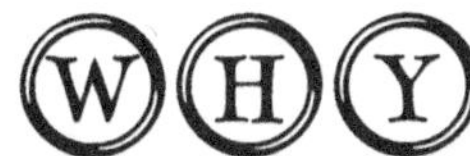

You want to turn your Viewers, Readers, Listeners into dedicated Fans from the get-go, don't you?

Then *ALWAYS* do your best. There are no if, ands, or buts on this one. Your Fans deserve it.

Don't you dare shortchange them, ever. You'll just end up shortchanging yourself, you know.

Consequently, take the time to ask more of yourself. Dig deep.

Then dig deeper.

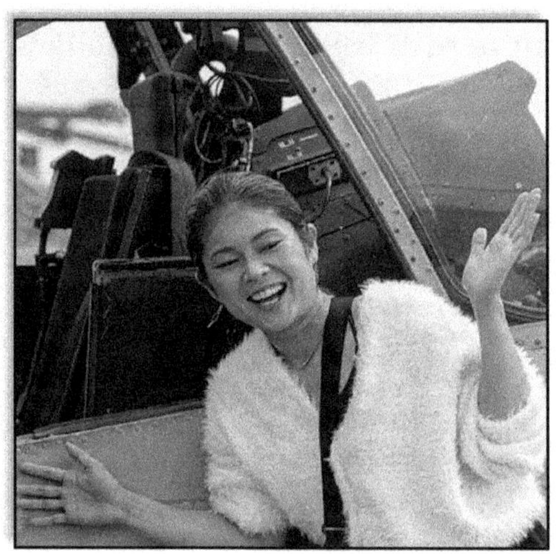

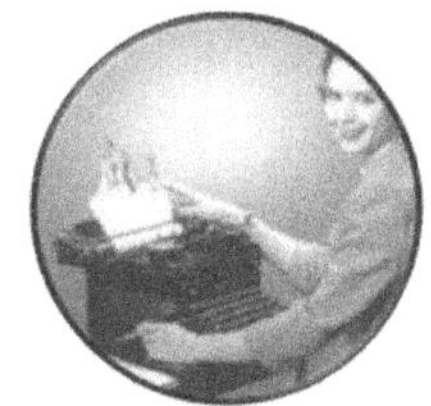

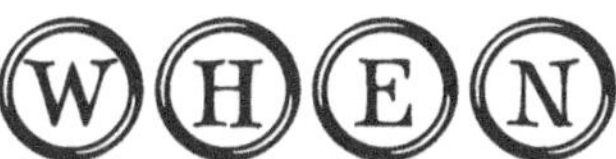

What are you waiting for, an engraved invitation? Now, Honey. Get to work on Your Bio now.

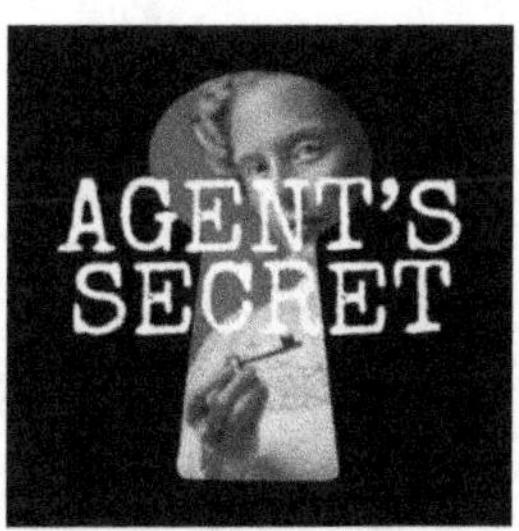

Those who hesitate are, indeed, lost.

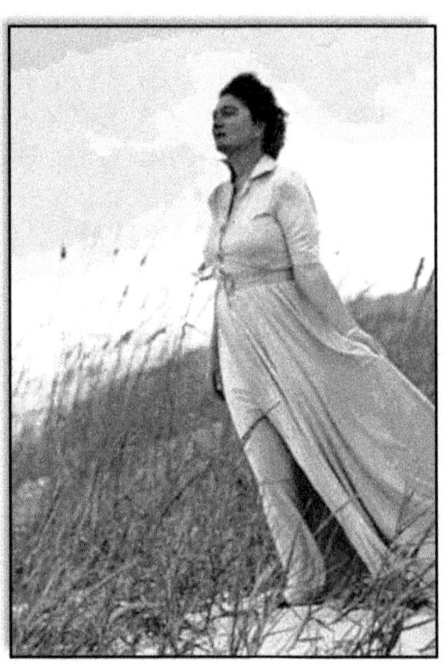

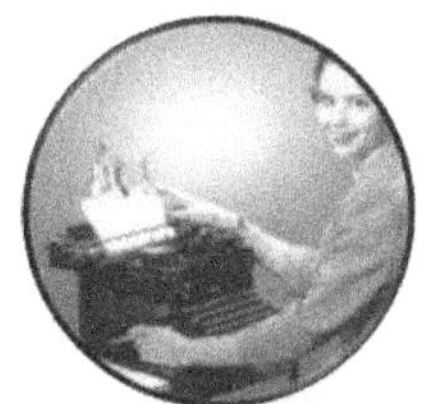

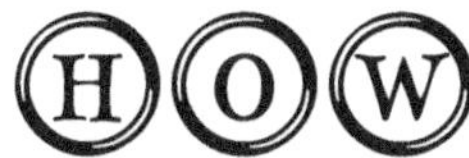

To make it easier for you to compose Your Bio, I've distilled everything into questions to ask yourself and dig deep to get details. Details that every Reader, Listener, Or Viewer would respond to and prompt them to then take action to connect with you.

If you spend time and think about these questions, you'll gather plenty of those juicy, relatable details to grab Readers, Viewers, and Listeners. Maybe you'll even think of some of your own that really speak of the True You expressed in Your Persona.

Plus, you'll be prepared to dodge every snag, obstacle, mess, predicament, glitch, and Catch-22 that flops in front of you, many before they even find you. You'll be able to sail above the headaches I've seen others trip over trying to tackle.

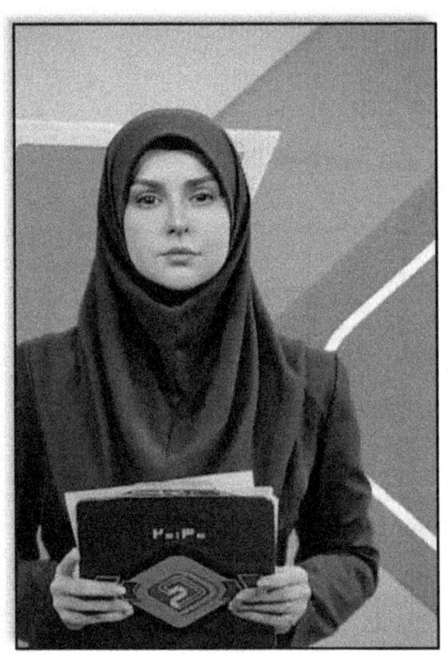

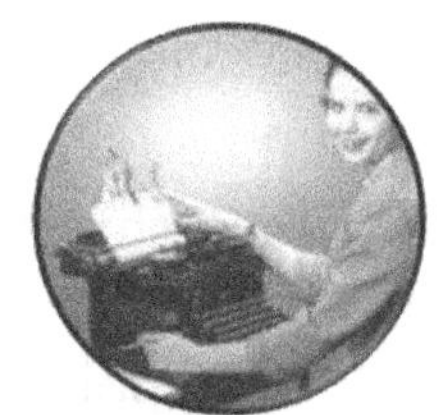

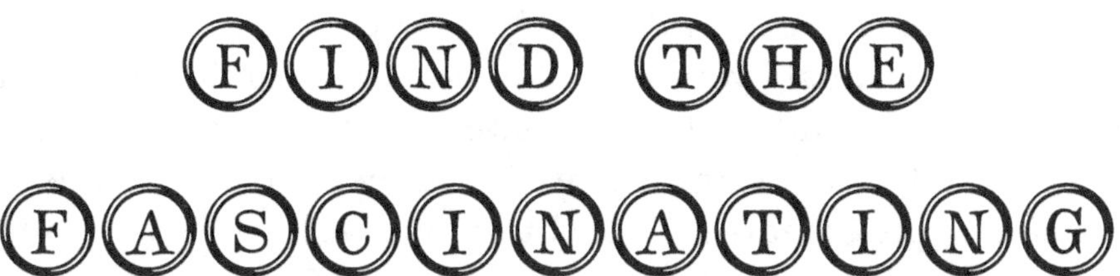

FIND THE FASCINATING

Think back a moment to those back-to-school vibes you had when you were a knobby-kneed little kid...

You sit at your desk your first day, your feet dangling in new shoes "with room to grow," classmates nervously rustling around you, a new teacher striding to the blackboard.

Excitement charges the crisp Autumn air. No one can be still.

You look down. Ah, there on your desk lies your new blue notebook and shiny yellow pencils strategically positioned in front of you, calming you. Your breath slows.

As you open the notebook you smell the new paper and newly-sharpened lead of your trusty #2 Dixon Ticonderoga. Ah-h-h-h-h.

Anticipation races through you. You can't wait to put pencil to paper.

Now is your opportunity to recapture that wonderful childhood feeling, that feeling of gaining confidence in yourself through answering simple questions. Work through them one at a time, jotting down as much as you can. You'll edit and polish it up later.

You'll see that, obviously, some questions just won't apply to you at all. Don't worry about it, but see which ones do and answer those as creatively as you can.

Really push yourself. Limber up your imagination. Kick slapdash, hit-and-run answers to the curb, Oh-Lazy-One. Bend your brain in new directions. This is a time to unleash your creativity, to bust out your free-wheeling, running-wild, gonzo, flat-out, to-the-max Muse.

Even try to answer some of the ones that just don't seem to apply to you at all, just to see what you turn up. You might be amazed.

To really get into it, on one of those pesky nights when you wake up unexpectedly for no damn reason, when your brain is still fuzzy, not fully engaged, pull out one or two of those challenging questions. In a dim light, scratch out answers without rereading what you've written. Then turn off the light and drift back to sleep. The next morning you may have gobbledy-gook, or you may have some bits that are surprisingly fabulous.

Once you've worked it all to a fine fare-thee-well you should have way more than you need. That's good. Overwriting is a plus here, as it gives you options. You want to be able to pick and choose from everything you've collected to select just the right combination of words – the ones that best showcase Your Persona. It's easier to write beyond what you need than it is to try to pad thin answers. We all know that padded, bloated text will stick out like a pig in a bedazzled silver lamé tutu.

When you've finished answering all the questions, you'll appreciate your strengths, realize how to set yourself apart, and see a clear focus of Your Persona for Viewers, Listeners, or Readers.

With this focus firmly under control, you can begin the satisfying process of pulling, poking, and prodding; slashing, slicing, and dicing; scratching, sorting, and shaping; collecting, cramming, and jamming; and then winnowing, molding, and polishing your answers into several versatile versions of Your Bio.

"I'm sorry, but all questions must be submitted in writing."
~ Willy Wonka,
Roald Dahl

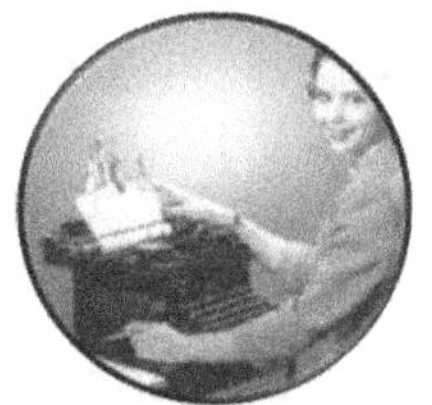

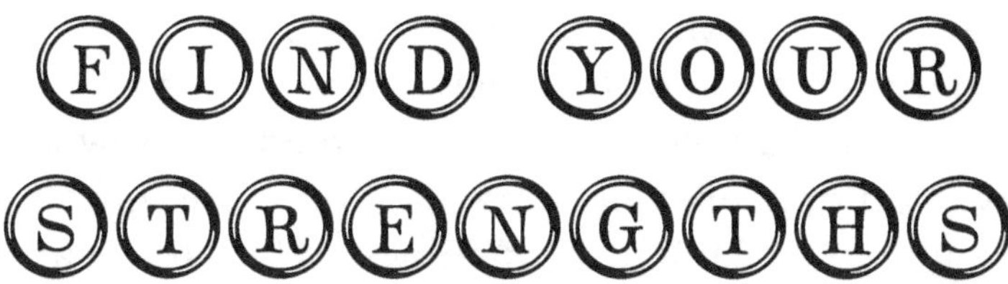

FIND YOUR STRENGTHS

1. What is your greatest strength? Asset?
2. What is most marketable about you?
3. What is very distinctive about you?
4. How do you differ from others doing the same thing?
5. Is it a combination of things that makes you unique?
6. Are you considered an expert in your field?
7. Do you hold advanced degrees in your field?
8. How long have you been in your field?
9. Have you won any nationally-recognized contests?
10. Have you received any nationally-recognized awards or grants?
11. Have you published any books? Who published them? How successful have they been?
12. Have you been featured in any articles? How many? Where?
13. Have you published any articles related to your work? How many? Where?
14. What are your current projects? At what stage are they?

15. Have you taught classes, led workshops, given speeches? Where? how many people? How long?
16. Have you had your own newspaper or magazine column? Local, regional, national, international? How many Readers?
17. Have you maintained a popular blog? Local, regional, national, international? How many subscribers?
18. What is your online reach with Fans? How many Readers, Viewers, or Listeners?
19. Do you have a following on social media? How large?
20. Have you appeared on a podcast, or a radio or TV show as a guest? What type of show? What size market?
21. Have you had your own podcast, or radio or TV show? What type of show? What size market?

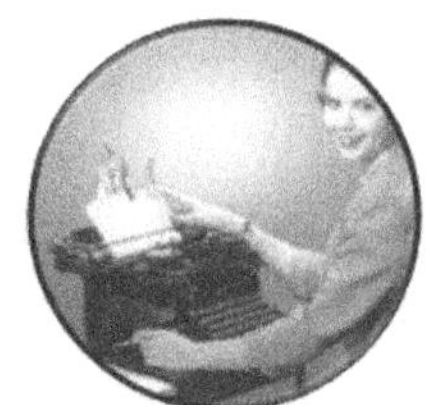

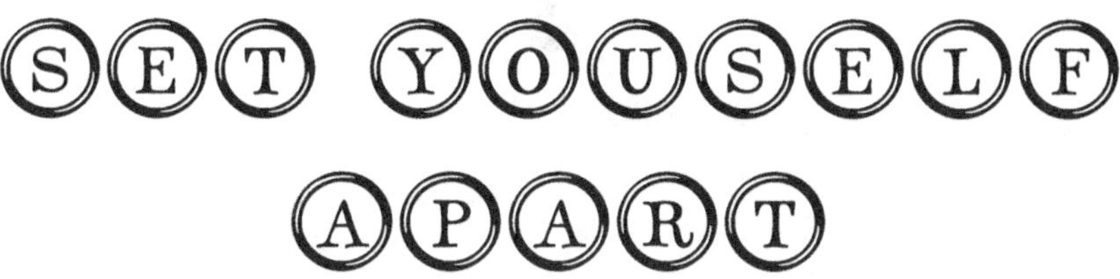

1. Where did you go to school? What kind of experience was it?
2. Have you lived in any exotic places? How did it affect you?
3. What fascinating or bizarre jobs have you held? Which was your favorite? Least favorite? Saddest? Yuckiest? Funniest? Why?
4. What jobs have you held that led you to what you do now? Any nationally known companies?
5. What have you done as a volunteer? How did you feel about that?
6. Do you own a business? What kind? Do you have any nationally known clients?
7. What do you have in common with what you do? How do you differ?
8. What are some of your most unusual accomplishments?
9. What are your loves? Your favorite pastimes?
10. What is your most dubious talent?
11. What kind of world did you grow up in?

12. What kind of world do you live in now?
13. Who's inspired you? Why? How?
14. What events have shaped you? Why? How?
15. How does today's world shape you every day?

In late night discussions with friends, maybe on a long road trip, around a campfire, or in the back of a bar, have you ever asked each other about the jobs you've held, all the weird stuff you've done for a buck? Some gigs for maybe only a day? What does your crazy list look like?

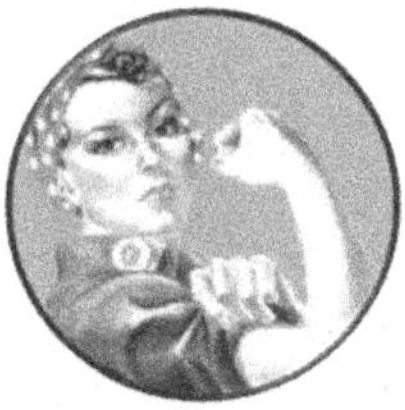

Here's mine (in no particular order): literary agent, speaker, website designer, magazine writer, photographer, screenwriter, ghostwriter, book producer, magazine editor-in chief, publisher, book designer, cover artist & designer, book editor, conference organizer, video producer, corporate writer, speech writer, business consultant, real estate broker, campaign manager, public relations director, event planner, sign painter, store owner, citrus packer & shipper, teacher, home designer & draftsman, carpenter, roofer, plumber, electrician, flooring installer, mason, tile installer, painter, driver, jewelry designer, artists' supply salesman, upholsterer, furniture refinisher, carpet cleaner, seamstress, artist, weaver, Girl Scout leader trainer, cook, retail store clerk, fashion warehouse worker, model, receptionist, musician & singer, camp counselor, tutor, golf tournament organizer, canoe instructor, switchboard operator, caterer, restaurant hostess, waitress, apartment rental manager, maid, nanny, orange juicer, golf course weed whacker, surfboard ding patcher, gold-embroidered satin tuxedo tailor, driving range ball girl, golf cart hustler, beer slinger, chicken fryer, chicken cutter, chicken liver packer.

All of which adds up to a fine writer's resume!

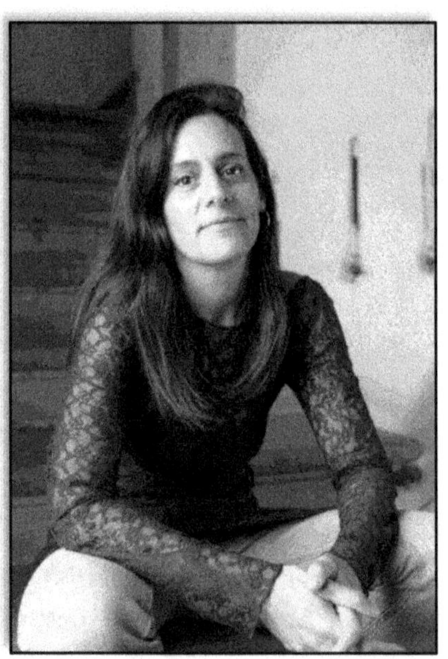

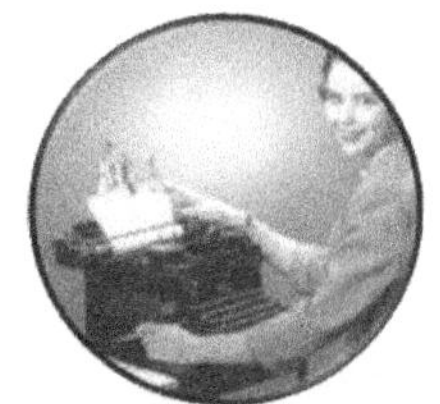

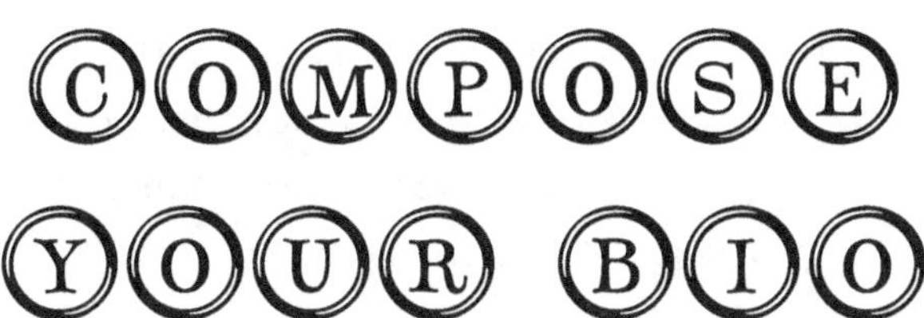

COMPOSE YOUR BIO

Your Bio is configured to promote and market you, but rarely can one Bio serve every need that might pop up. Above all, be honest. No padding. The object here is to present Your Persona in the most fascinating and marketable way, not puffed up beyond believability. And, trust me, Fans are so savvy these days, they can spot sincerity immediately, and pretense even quicker.

Take the first draft of Your Bio and shape it for versatility. One size does not fit all. Compose at least three Bios: one Long (250 words or less), one Short (100 words or less), and a handy Brief Bio (50 words or less).

Which Bio you will need for any situation – whether a Long, Short, or Brief Bio – will depend directly on the platform and their requirements. Comply with their conditions, or risk being ignored. If you're fortunate they'll have room for a Long Bio, but that's rare, so you'll need to rely on Your Short Bio and your hard-working Brief Bio.

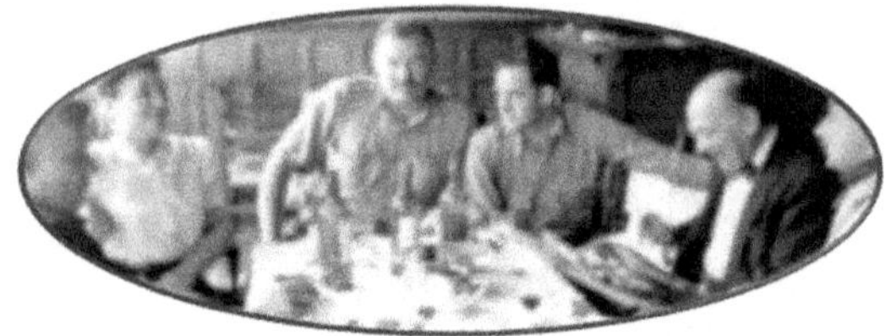

Once you have a Long Bio, cutting that down to a Short Bio can be tough, and cutting it down to a measly 50 words or less can be extremely trying. Here's one way to accomplish it: With a little help from your friends...

Invite a group over one evening to help. In exchange for their help, you'll provide the pizza and beer, Chinese take-out, or pinot noir and asiago and baguettes.

Have on the table a zillion copies of your double-spaced, Long Bio (lots of copies means lots to work with). Spread out pencils, note cards, red pens, highlighters, Post-it notes, scissors and tape, whatever you think might be helpful tools.

Then get the group discussing Your Bio in depth, prioritizing bits, and cutting out what they can live without (even though you may adore it), and maintaining only the juiciest stuff.

At the end of the evening, you'll have a Short and a Brief Bio you can live with, and one that fans will respond to. This method works every time. It might even deliver a great short Bio you might never have thought of, often with unusual combinations for energetic contrast.

For total flexibility, you can compose a Long, Short, and Brief Bio slanted to appeal directly to each segment of the market you're trying to reach. That way you'll be sure to have the perfect Bio for any situation that might pop up come tomorrow. You certainly don't want to be left hurrying and scurrying at the eleventh hour, trying to edit Your Bio down or slant it to a particular market.

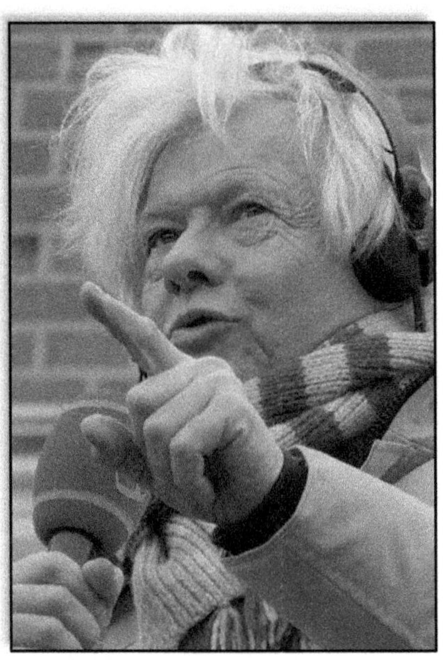

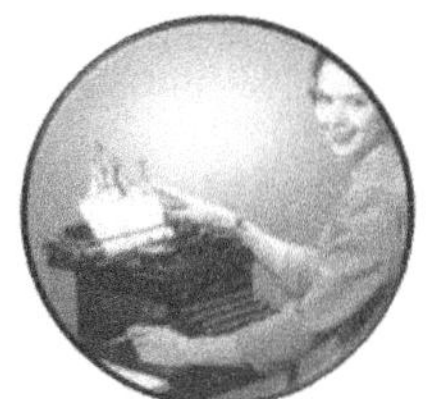

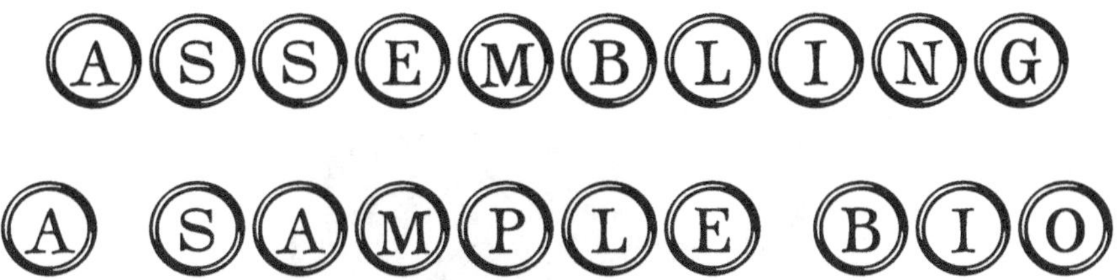

ASSEMBLING A SAMPLE BIO

Using a guinea pig from one of my workshops, I've included a sample of how one very inexperienced Writer took the questions and ran with them.

Patti (not her real name, naturally) laughed her way through writing out the answers to the questions, feeling there simply was no way to define her Persona and then make it interesting enough to Readers, let alone make her Persona compelling enough to turn them into Fans.

See for yourself.

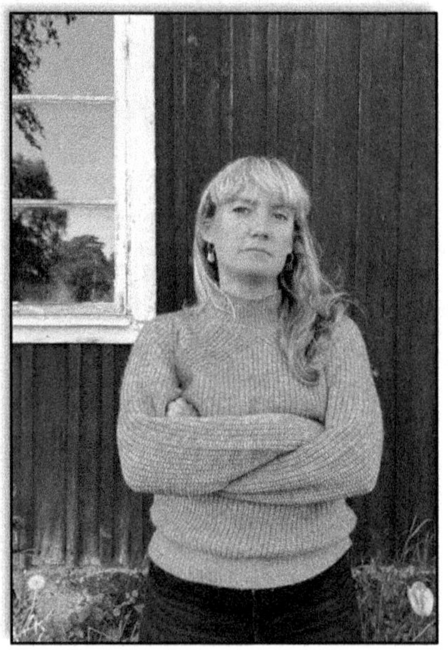

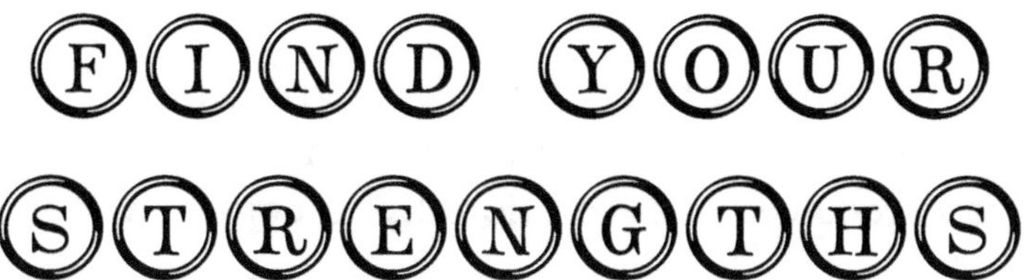

What is your greatest strength? Asset?

I have a deep and strong love of family, which permeates all my decisions. My family is my best asset, my most valuable possession, creation, ongoing project.

What is most marketable about you?

I always have a smile crossing my face. I'm casual, easy-going, likable, and laugh easily. At this stage of the game, there's very little that surprises me.

What is very distinctive about you?

I'm very short, barely five feet, with a contagious laugh. People lovingly call me an elf.

How do you differ from others with similar works?

I'm a raucous mama who has lived a normal-on-the-surface life that underneath isn't.

Is it a combination of things that makes you unique?

We're all a gumbo, aren't we?

Are you considered an expert in your field?

If the field is parenting, well, then, I'm a Ph.D.

Do you hold advanced degrees in your field?

Oh, yeah, certainly a Masters in Conquering Tantrums, Masters in Dating Advice, and with four daughters, a Doctorate in Wedding Planning.

How long have you been in your field?

Too long.

Have you won any nationally recognized contests?

No. But you have to enter to win, don't you?

Have you received any nationally recognized awards or grants?

Do they give out an award for Best Mother-of-the-Bride? Or grants for Making Baby Quilts?

Have you published any books? Who published them? How successful have they been?

Oh, how I wish. Then I'd have a better handle on this writing of books thing. But I've finished the first, *Sand in Biddy's Bathing Suit,* and started on the second, so I guess I have a series, maybe a Beach Biddy series.

Have you been featured in any articles? How many? Where?

I was interviewed for an article on being a Girl Scout leader where I extolled all the virtues.

Have you published any articles, etc? How many? Where? When?

I worked at a weekly newspaper years ago, doing every sort of odd job that the local beach paper required that week, from selling and collecting ads to writing obituaries, horoscopes, and a few features. I was often pressed into duty to cover a basketball game or city council meeting. Who could keep count?

What are your current writing projects? At what stage are they?

Besides this first novel, *Sand in Biddy's Bathing Suit,* I have the next in the series, *Looking in Biddy's Beach Bag,* started, and the third, *Under Biddy's Beach Umbrella,* outlined.

Have you taught classes, led workshops, given speeches? Where? How many people?

I taught workshops when I worked as a weight-loss counselor, regularly having 50-100 people in them. I always left them laughing and feeling good about themselves.

Have you had your own newspaper or magazine column? Have you maintained a popular blog? Local, regional, national, international? How many subscribers?

I was "Aunt Ada" in the "Ask Aunt Ada" relationship column for the local paper. Subscribers around 3,000. And what exactly is a blog?

What is your online reach with Fans? How many Readers, Viewers, or Listeners?

Let's see, "Ask Aunt Ada" does appear in the online version of the newspaper, and that has at least 100 times as many visitors as we have subscribers.

Do you have a following on social media? How large?

Oh, do you mean like Facebook or Instagram? My kids set it up for me so people can find me. I don't spend much time there. Guess I should.

Have you appeared on a radio or TV show as a guest? What type of show? What size market?

I appeared on local TV and radio when I was a weight-loss counselor. They liked my personality and sense of humor and had me back often.

Have you had your own radio or TV show? Podcast? What type of show? What size market?

What a fun idea. I'd love to do that. I can see it now: "Ask Aunt Ada" brought to life for young women today. A bit of dating advice, a dash of fashion, a splash of etiquette, a soupçon of style. Lots of attitude.

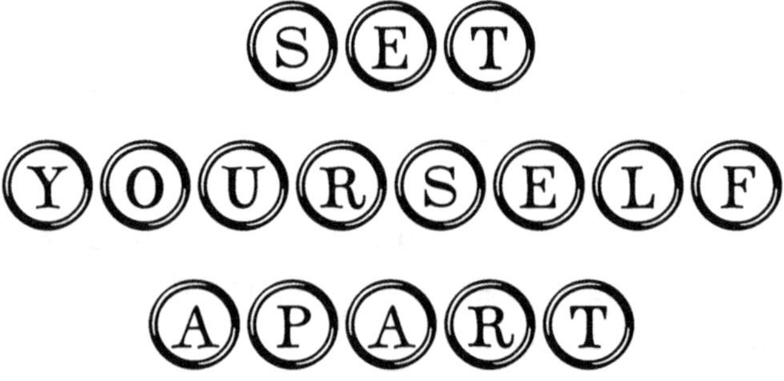

Where did you go to school? What kind of experience was it?

I grew up in a small Maine town and attended a high school with a graduating class of 23. There were more moose in town than graduates in my class.

Have you lived in any exotic places? How did it affect you?

The beach is where my second husband and I moved when it was a small, out-of-the-way place. My children were all small then, and it was a great place to let babies study seagulls and toddlers to run on the sand, and later for teenagers to sneak a first kiss in the moonlight, all not far from mom and dad. Currently, I live within sight of the Mississippi River and daily speculate on what the Big Muddy sees on its ramble to the sea.

What fascinating or bizarre jobs have you held? Which was your favorite? Least favorite? Saddest? Yuckiest? Funniest? Why?

Teach school. Teach? Hell, I spent most of my time trying to teach the kids how to save themselves from the world and keep them from killing each other. Oh, let's see, what are some of the odd jobs I've had? I've sold make-up door-to-door by bicycle, the youngest in a bicycle seat, one on a tricycle, and the two oldest on following on their bicycles. Did I mention being a mom? Definitely, the yuckiest. And favorite.

What jobs have you held that led you to what you do now? Any nationally known companies?

There's the "Ask Aunt Ada" column that made me sit my ass in a chair and write each day to make word quotas and deadlines.

What have you done as a volunteer? How did you feel about that?

Church choir director. Girl Scout Assistant Leader. The days in Scouts were some of the richest. And funniest.

Do you own a business? What kind? Do you have any nationally known clients?

When the girls were in high school I owned a fabric shop, but sold it when I realized I was working for less than I paid my employees. Either I was too good an employer or too poor an employee. Either way, I figured it meant I wasn't meant to be an entrepreneur.

What do you have in common with what you do? How do you differ?

Biddy and I are inseparable. She's the tiger that lives down deep inside me, she says what I'd never dare to. We're both gals who live to "go beach."

What are some of your most unusual accomplishments?

I've snorkeled in the Florida Keys, driven a big rig, survived a murder attempt, rescued my girls from a kidnapper, made quilts and teddy bears for appreciative little ones, peddled Girl Scout cookies, canoed amid alligators, taken a younger lover. But the best? That would be my four incredible daughters. They amaze me every day.

What are your loves? Your favorite pastimes?

Camping, reading, practicing Tai Chi, walking the beach, baking Christmas cookies with my daughters. We refer to ourselves as The Coven. Yeah, now that the grandchildren are old enough, we let them come and play in the dough, too, and spend the afternoon laughing.

What is your most dubious talent?

I can get down and boogie to the moldy oldie, "Bad, Bad Leroy Brown." It's a dancing tune I never, ever get tired of. That beat keeps me going, on through the night, no matter how tired I might be.

What kind of world did you grow up in?

I grew up in a time and place insulated from the world's harshness and hard edges.

What kind of world do you live in now?

It is a peaceful, yet jam-packed time, punctuated by grandbaby visits.

What authors have inspired you? Why? How?

Where to begin??? I'll come back to this.

What events have shaped you? Why? How?

You can't get to my stage in life without having so many extraordinary influential events that they would fill many pages.

Have you ever been featured in an article? Why? Where? When?

Counting that centerfold in Playboy last month?

&

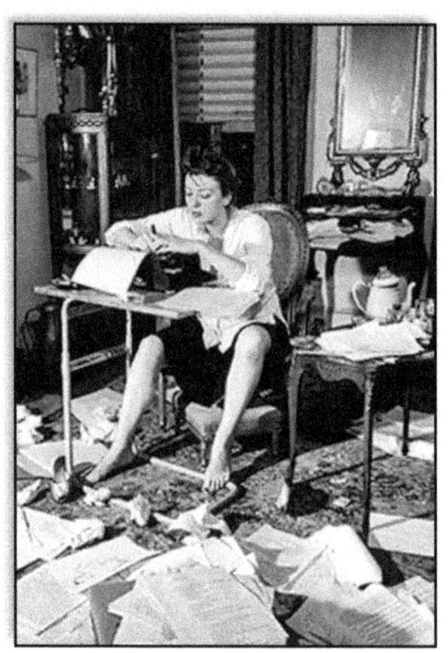

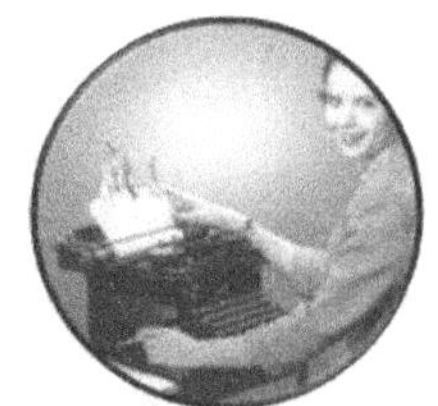

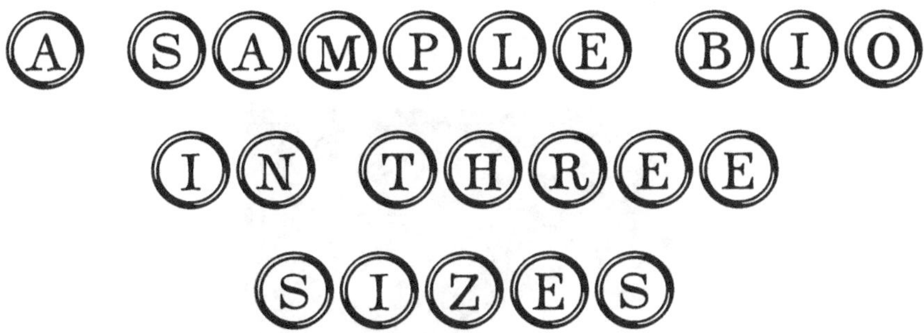

Patti astonished herself when she looked at her answers and could use them to craft three versatile versions of her Bio. And she thought it couldn't be done.

Note how she maintained focus on her Persona, taking the raw information in her off-the-cuff answers and shaping that, bit-by-bit, first into a Long Bio, then into a Short Bio, then narrowing it down to focus on just the juicy bits for her Brief Bio.

Lastly, she included a call to action by including her contact info for her website (naturally, in this case, not a real website).

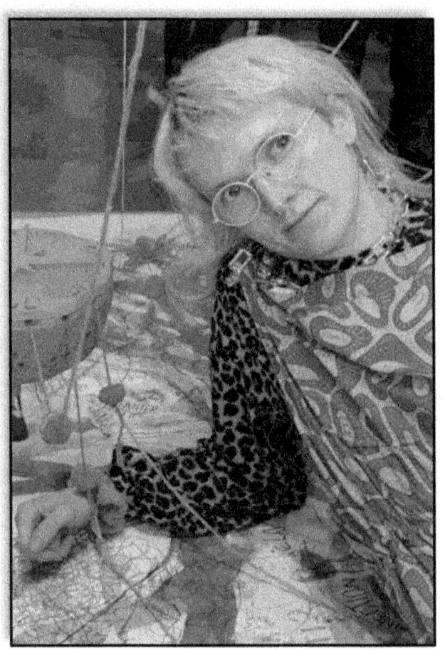

PATTI FLETCHER considers herself a raucous mama who's lived a normal-on-the-surface life, which underneath isn't. She's snorkeled in the Florida Keys, driven a big rig, rescued her daughters from a kidnapper, sold make-up by bicycle, made quilts, canoed amid alligators, survived a murder attempt, and taken a younger lover. Quick to smile, with a contagious laugh, by now there's very little that surprises such an elf.

Growing up in a time and place insulated from the world's hard edges, with more moose in town than high-school graduates, family permeates her world and her fiction. Her inspiration for *Sand in Biddy's Bathing Suit* is the out-of-the-way beach where she raised her four girls – an astonishing place to let toddlers study seagulls, kids play hopscotch in the sand, and teenagers sneak a first kiss.

With heavy time in the parenting trenches, Patti's also served as a teacher, choir director, Girl Scout leader, weight-loss counselor, shop owner, and her favorite, newspaperwoman. She sweated every job the beach paper required, from a splash of selling ads to a smidgen of covering a council meeting to a soupçon of writing obituaries, horoscopes, and "Ask Aunt Ada." Along the way she became a workshop leader and frequent TV and radio guest. She always left them laughing.

Following weekend forays to the beach she cranks up the music and digs down to the tiger inside her, working on upcoming works in the Beach Biddy Series, *Looking in Biddy's Beach Bag* and *Under Biddy's Beach Umbrella.*

www.BeachBiddy.com

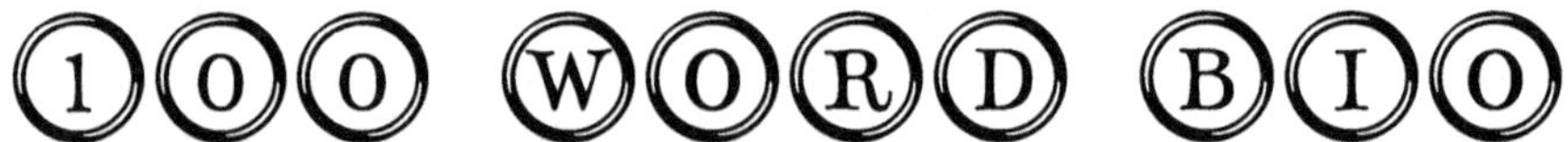

PATTI FLETCHER lives a normal-on-the-surface life, which underneath isn't. She's snorkeled the Florida Keys, rescued her daughters from a kidnapper, sold make-up by bicycle, made quilts, canoed amid alligators, been a newspaperwoman, taught school, survived a murder attempt, and taken a younger lover. Her inspiration for *Sand in Biddy's Bathing Suit* is an astonishing out-of-the-way beach where she raised her four girls. Quick to smile, with a contagious laugh, little surprises such an elf. Following forays to the beach Patti works on upcoming books in the Biddy Beach Series, *Looking in Biddy's Beach Bag* and *Under Biddy's Beach Umbrella.*

www.BeachBiddy.com

PATTI FLETCHER lives a normal/not-so-normal life, having snorkeled the Florida Keys, sold make-up by bicycle, rescued her daughters from a kidnapper, taught school, written for a newspaper, survived a murder attempt, and taken a younger lover. Quick to smile, with a contagious laugh, little surprises such an elf.

www.BeachBiddy.com

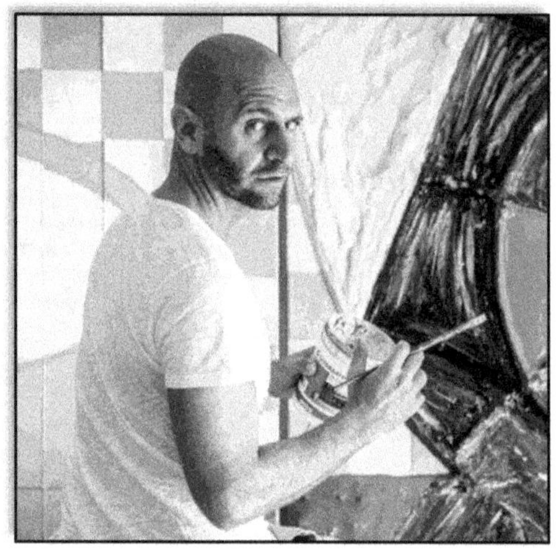

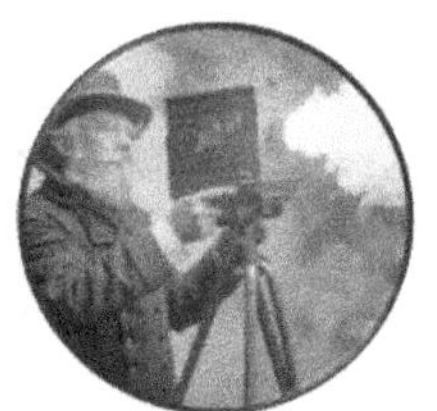

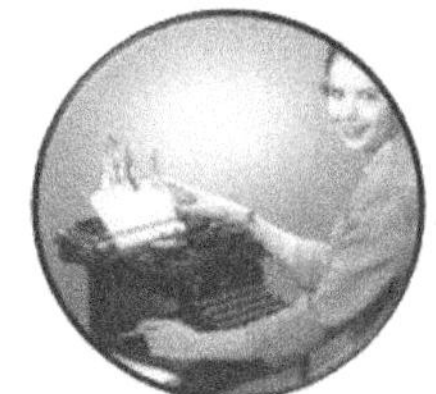

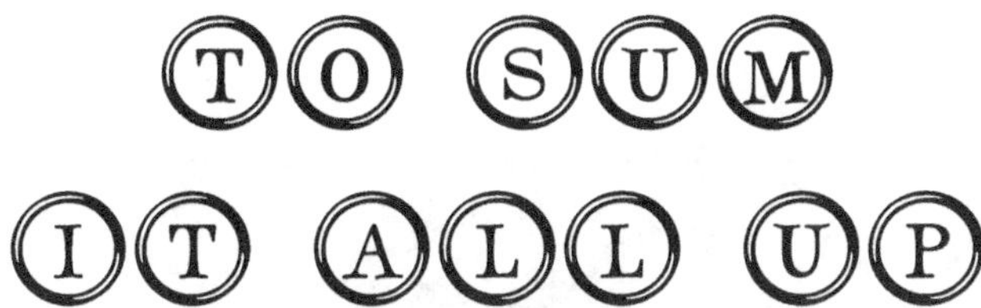

TO SUM IT ALL UP

You now possess an understanding of the importance of developing Your Persona, and shaping how you present yourself to the world through Your Photo and Your Bio, so you can grab Viewers, Listeners, Readers *BEFORE* they see your work.

You discovered how to fashion Your Photo and Your Bio so they are your handiest, major mondo, A-number-1, indispensable, legit, hardest-working secret weapons. How to perfect them into promoting pieces-of-wizardry. How to make them Major Monetizers with your Fans.

And isn't that what all of us with the gift of glorious gab seek? Tried-and-True Fans so that we can continue to do what we love?

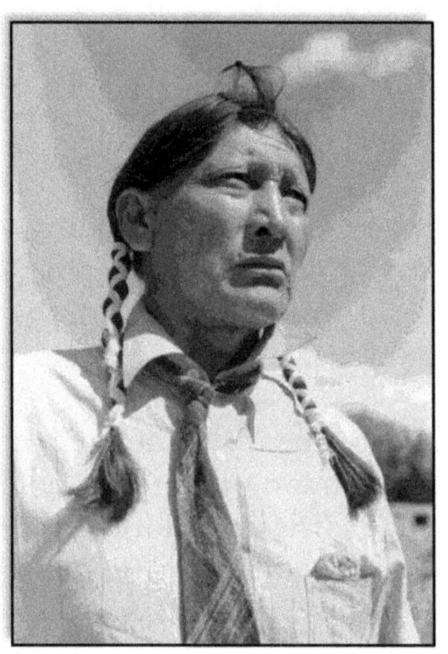

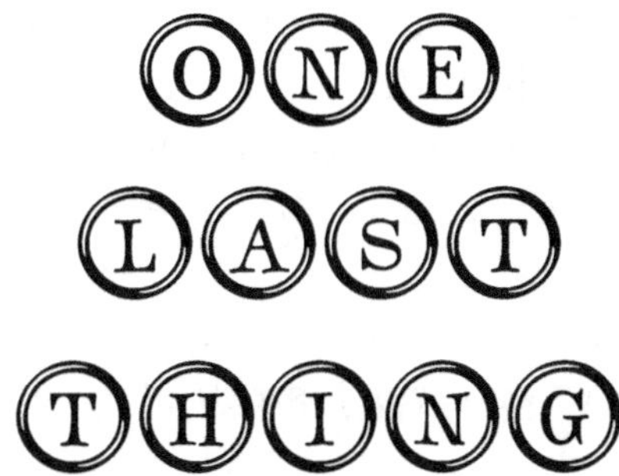

ONE LAST THING

Creative folk are incredibly benevolent people, sharing their knowledge of the craft and business, and life, with their comrades-in-arms as freely as they share their works with the world. I am truly grateful to have had the opportunity to learn in person at the feet of masters – my curiosity pushing me, their generosity pulling me.

Here are a few of those creative and generous folk who, when our paths crossed, impacted my world view from that point forward:

- Hugh Cave taught me Writers are ordinary lovable folk and oh-so-much more,
- Hank Leiferman made me realize I had valuable writing skills,
- Peter Matthiessen shared his peanut butter sandwich and the value of sharing knowledge, both to the giver and the receiver,

- Ernest Gaines shared a cold concrete step and literary lessons for hours,
- Jonathan Winters shared a cold concrete bench and life lessons for hours,
- Hiram Williams drilled into my head to pay attention to all the minutiae in everything you create, no matter how itsy-bitsy, because God really is in the details,
- Daniel Keyes talked to me about point-of-view until the lightbulb of full understanding came on,
- Les Standiford proved the value of story structure,
- Barbara Parker shared her method for bulletproofing a plot,
- Bebe Moore Campbell told me to look and listen, and open my eyes to layer a story like paint on a canvas to get richer colors,
- Arlo Guthrie told me to look and listen, and open my ears to layer a story to get richer colors,
- Diana Gabaldon illustrated to me elegance in story and craft,
- John Saul taught me that what all editors really want is a *good* story *well* told,
- Michael Connelly illuminated the power of a title operating on multiple levels to reflect the full story,
- Donald Maass encouraged me to hang on past the initial bumpy times,
- Ray Bradbury and Ben Bova both taught me to embrace the future,
- Bob Dylan revealed to me the joy in kicking back and enjoying the unexpected,
- David Hagberg taught me to dig deep, and then deeper yet, and welcome what I found,
- Anne Perry showed me the strength of grace – and the true gift of Christmas is peace,

- Leo Lyons showed me the power of listening to your own heart,
- Jack Whyte and James Patterson proved to me the value in being yourself,
- Martin Caidin proved to me the value in sometimes being someone else, especially on the page,
- Dave Barry taught me how to laugh with everyone,
- Stephen King taught me to laugh at myself.

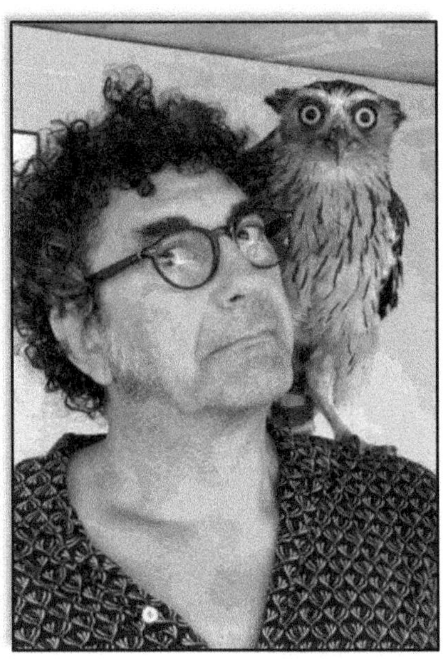

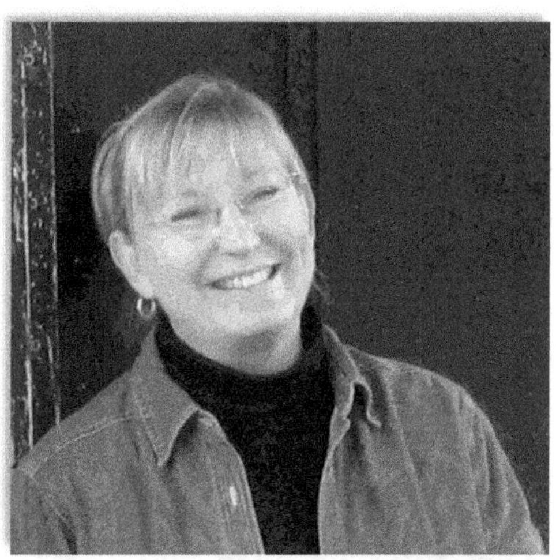

Cricket Freeman has always been a tenacious Southern broad who, once she shifted her creativity to the publishing world, ended up finding herself on all sides of the editorial desk at one time or another. It kicked off when a drunken bestselling author, a former editor, happened to grace her guestroom one summer and proclaim her a damn-fine writer, so Cricket began hammering out articles on a dusty Olympic typewriter for extra bucks. She kept chugging, taking on every paying gig she could scramble up.

As publishing opportunities opened and technology escalated through computers, websites, digital publishing, video, and streaming, she hung in, piling on credits by the pound, reviewing thousands of Photos and Bios, and accumulating multiple hats as she went: Writer, Literary Agent, Photographer, Editor, Speaker, Publisher, Ghostwriter, Literary Consultant, Magazine Editor-in-Chief , Writer's Retreat Host & Instructor.

Above all, she writes. She is a Word Warrior.

Subscribe to her blog: "Cricket Asks Writers: What If?"
AugustAgency.com/blog

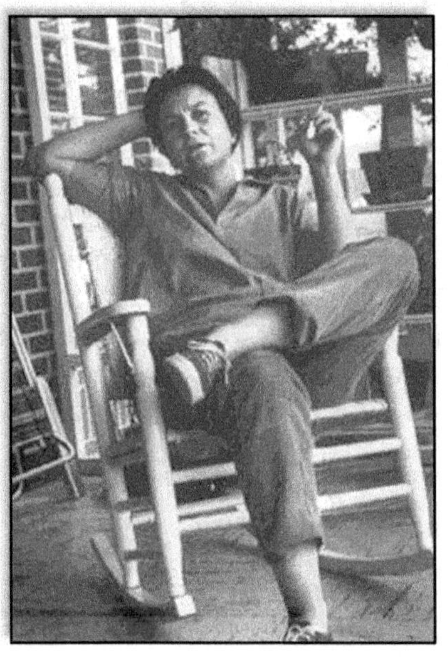

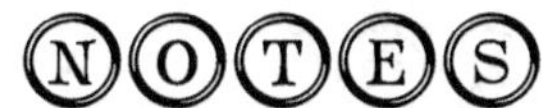

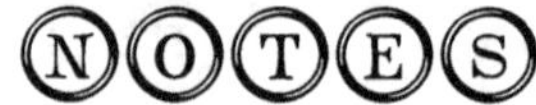

www.ingramcontent.com/pod-product-compliance
Lightning Source LLC
LaVergne TN
LVHW010102110826
845155LV00028B/452

* 9 7 8 1 9 4 2 0 1 8 2 1 6 *